THE DOCTRINE AND COVENANTS
AND THE FUTURE

The
Doctrine and Covenants and the Future

By

Roy W. Doxey

Dean, College of Religious Instruction
Brigham Young University

Published by
Deseret Book Company

1972

Printed by

DESERET NEWS PRESS

in the United States of America

Dedicated
To my wife, Alberta,
who has given
full cooperation
and support

PREFACE

Ancient prophets predicted the restoration of the gospel of Jesus Christ and the ushering in of the last and greatest dispensation of all times. It was known to them that in this dispensation "all things would be gathered together in one." Men and women living in this period are richly blessed in the greater knowledge and opportunities available for them to see the fulfillment of what the Lord has told His holy prophets would come to pass. Very much of what these prophets predicted has already been fulfilled in the restoration of the gospel. This points up the magnitude of the work established by Joseph Smith under divine guidance.

Yet, notwithstanding this fact, the revelations given to the Prophet Joseph Smith as contained in the Doctrine and Covenants, have not been given the attention they should receive by members of The Church of Jesus Christ of Latter-day Saints.

The importance of the Doctrine and Covenants cannot be over-emphasized in its message to Latter-day Saints and to the world. The title of this volume, *The Doctrine and Covenants and the Future,* emphasizes one of the significant purposes for which the Lord established His work on the earth in this culminating period of time.

The fact that the Lord put so much stress in the modern revelations about the times in which we live and the future has, in part, prompted me to write this book. In my opinion, this area of study—the immediate future and what is called life after death—constitutes one of the great contributions of these revelations and the teachings of the Presidents of the Church.

It is necessary that we know that these are the last days. Evidence presented in this book supports that revealed truth.

It also testifies to the divine mission of the Prophet Joseph Smith.

A greater knowledge of and evidence for life after death is possessed by Latter-day Saints. This is one of the rich blessings of this people. Increased knowledge and confirmation of one's faith brings closer adherence to the principles of the gospel. An awareness of this truth has also motivated me to write this book. To every Latter-day Saint the Lord has promised as the work of righteousness "peace in this world and eternal life in the life to come." (Doc. & Cov. 59:23.)

Encouragement to write this book has been given to me by my co-workers on the general board of the MIA, especially Ted Bushman and Pearl Bridge Johnson.

ROY W. DOXEY

TABLE OF CONTENTS

Chapter One
THE SETTING

Chapter Two
LOOK FORWARD FOR SIGNS

Chapter Three
"THIS IS A DAY OF WARNING"

Chapter Four
THE SECOND COMING OF CHRIST

Chapter Five
THE MILLENIUM

Chapter Six
THE SPIRIT WORLD

The Setting

The Doctrine and Covenants, as to scripture, constitutes the doctrinal and organizational foundation of the Church of Jesus Christ of Latter-day Saints in our period, because it contains God's message to this generation. It is a product of the restoration of the gospel of Jesus Christ, after that gospel had been lost for centuries to the inhabitants of the world.

A Unique Book

The Doctrine and Covenants is a unique book among all the books in the world. This is so because its author is Jesus Christ, with Joseph Smith as the mortal instrument in its production. It is not infrequent to read an expression with this meaning: "Listen to the voice of Jesus Christ, your Lord, your God, and your Redeemer." In the main other books of scripture are about man's experiences with God and His works.

The second fact which makes a unique book of the Doctrine and Covenants is its being a modern book of scripture. It is written to and for people who are living today. This book testifies to the truth that the Lord speaks today about present-day needs as much as other ancient books of scripture were written for the people of their day.

The Prophet Joseph Smith recorded that the conference of November, 1831, accepted the revelations as "the foundation of the Church in these last days, and a benefit to the world . . . therefore the conference voted that they prize the revelations to be worth to the Church the riches of the whole earth, speaking temporally."[1]

SOURCES OF INFORMATION

This series of chapters is confined, in the main, to the Doctrine and Covenants. Insofar as advisable, all reference material in these chapters will be taken from this book of revelations. Sometimes subject matter is drawn from other books of scripture and also from the writings of modern prophets, another rich source of inspiration. Occasionally confirmatory references to other sources are provided on certain points, but this is the exception rather than the rule.

THE SCRIPTURES AND THE FUTURE

Ancient and modern prophets have considered the scriptures as guideposts to living. One important phase of this is what the scriptures say of the future. President Brigham Young believed that the scriptures "are of great worth to a person wandering in darkness. They are like a lighthouse in the ocean, or a finger-post which points out the road we should travel. Where do they point? To the Fountain of light."[2] In

---

[1]Joseph Fielding Smith, *Teachings of the Prophet Joseph Smith*, p. 8.
[2]*Discourses of Brigham Young*, p. 196.

a similar way the prophetic scriptures are believed to be a "light that shineth in a dark place."[3]

Not only should the scriptures be a guidepost, but when divine prophecies are fulfilled they serve as an aid to faith. It is apparent that Jesus had this in mind when He said to His disciples:

> And now I have told you before it came to pass, that, when it is come to pass, ye might believe. (John 14:29.)

PRINCIPAL MESSAGES

In this book reference to and elaboration upon the principal purposes of the Doctrine and Covenants will be given. The very important objective and purpose, not stated below, of setting forth in plainness how man may receive salvation, although not neglected is not elaborated upon. We may consider that these messages are three:

I   A warning to the world.

II   The events of the future and man's destiny.

III   Evidence of the reality of the life beyond the grave.

THE LORD'S PREFACE

Introductory to a series where the Doctrine and Covenants is relied upon primarily for subject matter and in accord with message one, a brief analysis of Section One, known as the "Lord's Preface," is neces-

---

[3]II Peter, 1:19.

sary. This revelation, given in November, 1831, constitutes the Lord's explanation of the object of His work in the Dispensation of the Fulness of Times.

When a series of revelations had been brought together in a volume to be known as a Book of Commandments, consisting of 65 chapters, the Lord gave what He called "my preface unto the book of my commandments, which I have given them (my servants) to publish unto you, O inhabitants of the earth."[4] Since that day this revelation has been Section One in all editions of the Doctrine and Covenants.

In the verse just quoted it should be noted that this message is to go to the inhabitants of the earth:

> For verily the voice of the Lord is unto all men, and there is none to escape; and there is no eye that shall not see; neither ear that shall not hear, neither heart that shall not be penetrated
>
> And the rebellious shall be pierced with much sorrow; for their iniquities shall be spoken upon the housetops, and their secret acts shall be revealed.
>
> And the voice of warning shall be unto all people, by the mouths of my disciples, whom I have chosen in these last days.
>
> And they shall go forth and none shall stay them, for I the Lord have commanded them. (Doc. & Cov. 1:2-5.)

THE PREFACE PROPER

With this introduction, the Lord proceeds to set forth the message or purpose of His revealed will in

---

[4] Doc. & Cov. 1:6.

these last days.[5] For the purpose of understanding
the contents of this preface, the following series of
questions and answers is given:

*What power will be given to those who carry the
message of this dispensation?* (vs. 8-10.)

    a.   To seal both on earth and in heaven the be-
        liever and the unbeliever unto the day of
        judgment.

    b.   The Lord will come to recompense to all ac-
        cording to their works.

*Why is the Lord's message directed to this genera-
tion?* (vs. 11-16.)

    a.   In preparation for the second coming of Christ.
    b.   Apostate condition of the world.
    c.   Men have set up their own gods.

*Through whom is the Lord's message to go to the
world and what can result from it?* (vs. 17-23.)

    a.   Joseph Smith was called of God.
    b.   The message is given that:

        1.   Men will not rely upon their fellow men,
            but upon the Lord.

        2.   Faith might increase through the restora-
            tion of the gospel.

*What purposes have the revelations served in the
lives of the men called into the Lord's service?* (vs. 24-
28.)

---

[5]*Ibid.*, 1:8-36.

a. That they might come to an understanding; that their errors might be corrected; that when they sought wisdom it was given; that if they sinned they might be chastened; and they might be made strong in their humility.

What powers have been received by His servants for the benefit of the world? (vs. 29-30.)

a. The power to translate the Book of Mormon.
b. The power to receive revelations and commandments.
c. Power to bring forth "the only true and living Church upon the face of the whole earth."

Why is it necessary to obey the commandments? (vs. 30-33.)

a. As individual members of the Church there is much to be desired in keeping the commandments, but as a group the Lord is pleased.
b. Sin is not condoned.
c. The sinner receives forgiveness by his repentance, but if he repents not the Spirit of the Lord is withdrawn.

Since the Lord has said that His message will go to all men, what final message does He want them to know? (vs. 34-36.)

a. The Lord is no respecter of persons.
b. Peace is to be taken from the earth.
c. Judgments await the world.
d. The Savior will surely come to reign.

Section One, or the Lord's Preface, is concluded with the definite assurance that what has been given will all be fulfilled and that the Spirit of God bears witness that "the record is true." (vs. 37-39.)

This "voice of warning" to the world is detailed in many of the revelations. Chapters Two, Three, and Four are about message one—a warning to the world. One can readily recognize from the revelation already printed that this message is of great importance to every Latter-day Saint. The Lord intended that His people should know of judgments to come and that the world might also have His warning message.

President Joseph Fielding Smith gave the following statement regarding the world today:

> In regard to the wars now raging on the earth, I am sure the prophets have spoken of them. The Lord told Joseph Smith that the war between the states commencing with the rebellion of South Carolina, was the beginning of the end. At that time peace was taken from the earth, and the prediction was made that beginning at that place, eventually war would be "poured out" upon all nations, bringing misery, death, mourning, famine, plague, earthquake, vivid lightnings, etc., causing the "inhabitants of the earth to be made to feel the wrath, and indignation, and chastening hand of an Almighty God, until the consumption decreed hath made a full end of all nations." It appears that now this is in course of fulfillment. (Joseph Fielding Smith, *Take Heed to Yourselves!* [Deseret Book Company, Salt Lake City, Utah], p. 180.)

By the way of information about the remaining chapters in this series, covering the other two principal messages of the Doctrine and Covenants, the following by President Joseph F. Smith is pertinent:

> I say to my brethren that the Book of Doctrine and Covenants contains some of the most glorious principles ever revealed to the world, some that have been revealed in greater fulness than they were ever revealed before to the world; and this, in fulfillment of the promise of the ancient prophets that in the latter times the Lord would reveal things to the world that had been kept hidden from the foundation thereof; and the Lord has revealed them through the Prophet Joseph Smith. (*Gospel Doctrine,* p. 45.)

The clarity with which this modern book of scripture confirms ancient truths and gives more enlightenment about the events of the future emphasizes its value to this generation. For one who is curious about future events, the Doctrine and Covenants will satisfy curiosity. But for the sincere truth-seeker about the future there are, of course, much greater rewards. In the last analysis, it is he who believes that receives most.[6]

------

[6]Doc. & Cov. 6:5-7; 11:22-27; Alma 12:9-11.

CHAPTER TWO

LOOK FORWARD FOR SIGNS

Of the many prophecies concerning the days in which we live and the future, the references in the Doctrine and Covenants to the last days seem to be the most numerous. The reason for this is the fact that we are living in the last dispensation, when the Lord's work "shall be cut short in righteousness."[1]

A TEST

A simple way to verify this statement is to open the Doctrine and Covenants at random a number of times, perhaps to twenty different pages, and read each page selected. It is probable that the majority of pages will contain references to the nearness of the Lord's coming, judgments on the wicked, signs of the last days or related ideas. A more impressive and accurate test would be to read the book from cover to cover and note the emphasis which is put by the Lord upon the fact that these are the last days.

Even among many Latter-day Saints the idea seems to be present that signs of the Lord's second coming are not too apparent or that it doesn't matter. The remark is often made that "I have heard of these things for so long, and nothing has happened."

---

[1]Doc. & Cov. 84:97.

THE LORD SPEAKS

A direct statement of the Lord about the signs of the latter days, however, sets forth their importance.

> And it shall come to pass that he that feareth me shall be looking forth for the great day of the Lord to come, even for the signs of the coming of the Son of Man. . . .
>
> And he that watches not for me shall be cut off. (Doc. & Cov. 45:39, 44; also 39:23.)

This warning is for all who profess belief in the divine origin of the work established by the Prophet Joseph Smith. Of those who are not "looking forth for the coming of the Son of Man," the Prophet said, "We shall be among those who are calling for the rocks to fall upon them."[2] The allusion to the latter part of this quotation refers to the wicked.[3]

Similar warnings have been addressed to all people who may hear the message from ancient or modern scripture. The voice of the Lord is unto all people and the means of proclaiming His message have been greatly increased by newspaper, radio, and the recently perfected television. This warning message is necessary because the world has strayed away from His teachings. Observe how explicit the modern revelation is on this point:

> Wherefore the voice of the Lord is unto the ends of the earth, that all that will hear may hear:

---

[2]Joseph Fielding Smith, *Teachings of the Prophet Joseph Smith*, p. 160.
[3]Revelation 6:12-17.

Prepare ye, prepare ye for that which is to come,
for the Lord is nigh;

And the anger of the Lord is kindled, and his sword
is bathed in heaven, and it shall fall upon the inhabitants of the earth.

And the arm of the Lord shall be revealed: and the
day cometh that they who will not hear the voice of the
Lord, neither the voice of his servants, neither give
heed to the words of the prophets and apostles, shall be
cut off from among the people;

For they have strayed from mine ordinances, and
have broken mine everlasting covenant. (Doc. & Cov.
1:11-15.)

Because of this apostate condition, the Lord gave
this evaluation of conditions in the world:

They seek not the Lord to establish his righteousness, but every man walketh in his own way, and after
the image of his own God, whose image is in the likeness of the world, and whose substance is that of an
idol, which waxeth old and shall perish in Babylon,
even Babylon the great, which shall fall. (*Ibid.,* 1:16.)

DECREASE IN FAITH

In general the people of over a century ago relied
more than now upon the Bible as a divine revelation,
though they did not have the true gospel of Jesus
Christ and the priesthood by which to represent the
Lord. Since then the scientific method of inquiry has
profoundly influenced the thinking of the Christian
clergy. "The authority of the Bible became untenable
in the traditional sense," wrote Professor Edward
Scribner Ames of the University of Chicago because

of the higher criticism of the scriptures.[4] These criticisms have had their effect upon the Christian clergy. The modernist school of thought "accepts to some extent the higher criticism, and evolution, but hold to theistic ideas of God and to some form of divinity of Christ, and to the authority of the Bible. The leading theological schools of America are certainly modernist in this sense."[5]

The trend toward liberalism began a few decades ago according to Professor Ames:

> Within the last five years, books have been published by theologians treating of the idea of God which would not have been tolerated in any Protestant seminary twenty years ago. A study of the views of five hundred ministers in and around Chicago, and of two hundred theological students, indicates a drift toward more radical thought among the younger men. Seventy-seven per cent of the ministers accepted the New Testament as an absolute and infallible standard of religious belief, but only thirty-three per cent of the students agreed. Half of the ministers believed in the story of the Creation in Genesis, but only five per cent of the students did so. One-third of the ministers and three-fourths of the students held that the Bible was no unique inspiration and did not believe in the occurence of miracles. Half of the ministers and nine-tenths of the students held that, in order to be a Christian, it was not necessary to participate in any sacraments, believe in the virgin birth, or hold membership in any church. (*Modern Trends in World Religions,* p. 31.)

---

[4]A. Eustace Haydon (Editor), *Modern Trends in World Religions,* p. 27.
[5]*Ibid.,* p. 30.

The change in religious beliefs, according to one writer, is due to a change in men's belief regarding God. Bishop Victor L. Brown, in the April 1970 General Conference, quoted the following from the *Reader's Digest*, March 1970:

> "I agree with David Klein ("Is There a Substitute for God?") that this moral erosion started when 'western man began to lose his belief in God as a personal force as decider of his fate, as ultimate judge of his actions. The idea that God created man became old fashioned; we evolved. . . . Life began to be seen as more or less accidental; sin became relative, sociological matter, and to many a pure fiction. . . . He still believed in right and wrong, and he still knew when he was doing wrong . . . but he no longer believed he had offended God by it or incurred His punishment. . . .
>
> 'The difference between living this way, and trying to live righteously because God commands it is profound.
>
> 'What used to be an offense against God became 'anti social'; a sin became a crime. . . . Stealing was bad because honesty was the best policy. You tried to avoid being unfaithful to your mate because it might harm your relationship. If you attended religious services, it was to respect tradition. Virtue became its own inexplicable reward, for there was no other.'" (p. 32.)

RELIGIOUS BELIEFS—THEIR MEANING

Many surveys on religious attitudes have been conducted in recent years, two of which are referred to by Henry C. Link,[6] which show that in the United

---

[6]Henry C. Link, *The Way to Security*, p. 213.

States 95 per cent of the people believe in God. One of these surveys was analyzed by three leading theologians—a Protestant, a Catholic, and a Jew. These are some of their conclusions, which point up the fact that profession of belief in God does not necessarily influence the daily lives of people:

> Most Americans regard religion as a private, painless pathway to heaven.
>
> Nearly three-quarters of them do not think of God as having any intimate relation to their daily life.
>
> Nearly three-quarters do not consciously connect their religion with their judgments of right and wrong.
>
> Religious education in America ends in the elementary stage. College students get adult education in the secular field, but only infant education in the religious field.

Another indicator of this fact was recorded recently. The following excerpt is taken from an article "Why Churches are Worried" from the March 19, 1970, issue of the *U. S. News and World Report:*

> The proportion of U. S. adults belonging to churches has been declining slowly but steadily since reaching a peak of 68% a dozen years ago. Now the Gallup Poll puts the figure at 63%. Church attendance at least once a week considered a more accurate barometer of the country's religious mood, has dropped from a record 49% in 1958 to 42% at present.
>
> Over all, church membership and attendance in the U. S. still are much higher than in Britain and some other Western nations. But belief strengthens among religious scholars that many Americans continue to attend church almost as a civic duty, not as a deeply felt

response to religious convictions or a desire to find ultimate meanings in their lives.

This type of secularist is still being heard from, especially in the upper ranks of churches and church groups. Recently, an outspoken radical, the Rev. James D. Watson, became moderator of the New York City presbytery of the United Presbyterian Church. He summed up his view of the church's mission as follows: "I see the ministry in terms of social action, not in terms of preaching or the rest of the nonsense we went through years ago. In our day, we are more concerned about man than God. God can take care of himself."

IN THE IMAGE OF HIS OWN GOD

In analyzing present conditions, Mr. Link believes that they are the result of our great material progress resulting in a whole collection of false theories and beliefs. These have become our new gods. Among these false gods is the false god of public education from which God has been systematically eliminated; and the theories of science which run counter to the revealed word of God. In the mechanistic theory of science, man is said to be the helpless victim of his environment and therefore free from sin, because men are not free agents.[7]

Men have set up their own gods at whose shrines they worship, which shall perish.[8] It seems that men have placed more trust in their own ability and less in the Giver of life. Many feel that the restrictions of

---

[7]For additional discussion of the false gods of today, one should read the final chapter of *The Way to Security*.

[8]Doc. & Cov. 132:13-14.

church membership are not conducive to a "free" life they believe to be most important. Indifference to church membership and to religious principles is a major sin today.

A recent poll indicates that three Americans in four say religion is losing influence on American life. In fact, in 1957, 14% so indicated; but in 1970, 75% believe this to be true.[8a]

PROPHECIES FULFILLED

That we are in the last days, the Lord has repeatedly declared.[9] It is the last time laborers are to be called into the vineyard[10] "that it may be pruned for the last time."

Numerous Bible prophecies concerning the restoration of the gospel and the Church in the latter days have already had their fulfillment. The coming of an angel from heaven with the everlasting gospel "in the hour of God's judgment" was fulfilled in the visitation of Moroni to Joseph Smith.[12] The "everlasting gospel" in the form of the Book of Mormon was foreknown as an event of the last days.[13] The restoration of the Holy Priesthood[14] and the establishment of the Church were to be a part of the last days.[15]

8a*U.S. News and World Report*, p. 45.
9Doc. & Cov. 1:4; 20:1; 27:6, 13.
10*Ibid.*, 33:3; 88:84.
11*Ibid.*, 39:17; 95:4.
12Rev. 14:6, 7; Doc. & Cov. 27:5.
13Isa. 29; Ezek. 37:15-28.
14Mal. 3:1-4; Doc. & Cov. 13; 27:7, 8.
15Dan. 2; Doc. & Cov. 65:2; 20:1.

Elijah's coming was to be "before the coming of that great and dreadful day of the Lord."[16]

Lord's Coming Near

When Elijah came to the Kirtland Temple, April 3, 1836, the Lord said that "by this ye may know that the great and dreadful day of the Lord is near, even at the doors."[17] That day—the second coming of Christ—is also called the "great day of the Lord."[18] The "last days" are those which precede His coming and which began in the days of the Prophet Joseph Smith.

When Moroni visited Joseph Smith, September, 1823, he said that some of the Biblical prophecies of the Lord's coming[19] were "not yet fulfilled, but was (were) soon to be."[20] Following this, he informed Joseph Smith "of great judgments which were coming upon the earth, with great desolations by famine, sword, and pestilence; and that these grievous judgments would come on the earth in this generation."[21]

Because of the use of the word "generation" in the modern scriptures in relation to the last days, a comment upon it may be useful.[22] It is apparent that the word does not always mean a certain number of years, as a hundred years, but rather a period of indefinite

---

[16]Mal. 4:5, 6; Doc. & Cov. 2; 110:13-16.
[17]Doc. & Cov. 110:16.
[18]Ibid., 43:17, 20-22; 45:39; 49:24.
[19]Acts 3:22, 23; Joel 2:28-32.
[20]P. of G. P., Joseph Smith 2:40, 41.
[21]Ibid., 2:45.
[22]Doc. & Cov. 84:4; 31; 45:30, 31.

length characterized by certain events.[22a] This definition is in accord with what the Lord told Joseph Smith,
that "this generation shall have my word through
you."[23] This obviously means the people of the Dispensation of the Fulness of Times.

A PARALLEL

Of all revelations in the Doctrine and Covenants,
Section 45 gives the most complete information of the
signs of the last days. This section and Matthew
Chapter 24 parallel each other, but the modern revelation gives some additional information.

In the New Testament chapter (consult the revi-
sion by the Prophet Joseph Smith, Pearl of Great Price,
Joseph Smith 1:4, where greater clarity exists), the
disciples asked Jesus: "Tell us, when shall these things
be which thou hast said concerning the destruction of
the temple, and what is the sign of thy coming, and of
the end of the world, or the destruction of the wicked,
which is the end of the world?" In 1831, the Lord
informed Joseph Smith that, as He had told His dis-
disciples anciently of the signs of His second coming in
glory, He would show these things plainly to him.[24]

In both places the events first mentioned[25] pertain
to the generation of Jews living in the time of Jesus
and the Apostles. These events were fulfilled by 70

[22a]Matthew 12:39.
[23]*Ibid.*, 5:10.
[24]Doc. & Cov. 45:15, 16.
[25]Matt. 24:1-20; Doc. & Cov. 45:15-24.

A.D. with the destruction of the temple and Jerusalem by the Roman army under the command of Titus. The second series of events are of the generation in which we live, the Dispensation of the Fulness of Times.[26]

Signs Summarized

In other revelations one finds confirmation of many of these events and conditions, although expressed, sometimes, in more vivid language. These references are also given in the summary below:

The preaching of the fulness of the gospel.[27] With the restoration of the Gospel, The Church of Jesus Christ of Latter-day Saints has undertaken to acquaint the world with its message. By modern agencies such as newspapers, radio, magazines, books, tracts, etc., in addition to personal contacts by missionaries, the message has gone out to the world.

The gathering of Israel[28] is now taking place. The Jews are returning to their modern state of Israel and for over 140 years people have accepted the gospel and have thereby come out of spiritual Babylon, the wicked world. Latter-day Saints have been gathering to Zion or America during this period of time. The ten tribes are yet to be restored.

Wars and rumors of wars. (See next chapter.)

Wickedness.[29]

---

[26]Matt. 24:21-35; Doc. & Cov. 45:25-42.
[27]Matt. 24:31; Doc. & Cov. 45:28, 29; 133:37.
[28]Matt. 24:27, 37; Doc. & Cov. 45:25, 43; 43:24.
[29]Matt. 24:30; Doc. & Cov. 45:27.

Earthquakes.[30] The destructiveness of this pheno-menon has been very great each year.

Unusual manifestation of heavenly bodies.[31] Comets and meteoric showers are some of these manifestations. It appears that there will be many more spectacular demonstrations of the power of God.

Plagues and diseases are spoken of in these words:

> And there shall be men standing in that generation, that shall not pass, until they shall see an overflowing scourge; for a desolating sickness shall cover the land. (Doc. & Cov. 45:31.)
>
> For I, the Almighty, have laid my hands upon the nations, to scourge them for their wickedness.
>
> And plagues shall go forth, and they shall not be taken from the earth until I have completed my work, which shall be cut short in righteousness. (*Ibid.,* 84:96-97.)

Although there have been diseases and plagues in the world almost since the beginning, it seems that new diseases appear as others are brought under control. An awareness of the extent of just what is happening in the world today will show that regardless of the wonderful achievements of medical science, the world is still very much sick. Plagues and desolating sickness are rampant. This is well illustrated in an article in the *United Nations World,* June, 1952, entitled "Why the World Is Sick." This article sets forth the magnitude of the job before the world in alleviating suffering and curing disease. Beginning with this

---

[30]Matt 24:29; Doc. & Cov. 45:33; 88:89.
[31]Matt. 24:33; Doc. & Cov. 45:40-42; 88:87; 29:14.

definition of health, "a state of complete physical, mental, and social well-being," the assertion is made that "the entire world is sick."

> On the one hand are the "mass" diseases, terrible parasitic and infectious cripplers which play havoc with the lives and happiness of two-thirds of the earth's inhabitants. On the other are the "luxury" diseases, such as cancer, which have appeared in the western world as the mass diseases have been conquered. Both of these must be eliminated or controlled before the immeasurable rewards of global health can be enjoyed.
>
> The luxury diseases are in many ways the most fascinating and challenging. As the jungle of mass diseases —plague, typhus, leprosy, cholera—was cleared away in the West, new sicknesses, more refined but equally deadly, sprang into view. (p. 32.)

Among the "luxury" or "more refined" diseases which afflict people in the well-off nations of Europe and America, some have their origin in conflicts and anxieties, giving peptic ulcers, alcoholism, arteriosclerosis, and mental illness. It is reported by the National Association for Mental Health that one of every twelve children born this year in the United States will require hospitalization at some time during life as a result of mental ill-health. Cancer and poliomyelitis seem to be the truest examples of the "luxury" class.

The "mass" diseases are those which affect, disable, or kill substantial proportions of the people in the area attacked. Among these is malaria, which attacks 300,000,000 people in the world, while tuberculosis, which is even more widespread, causes more deaths than malaria· "Yaws is perhaps the most hideous of the mass diseases. Similar to syphilis, it cripples, disfigures, and debilitates victims of all ages. . . . Estimates put the number of people whose lives are being ruined by syphilis as high as 100 million. In some areas seven out of every ten people are infected· Among women with syphilis who have never had treatment, the number of known conceptions which result in miscarriages, stillbirths, and syphilitic babies has been recorded as 83 per cent. Gonorrhea may infect as many as 300 million people."[32] Trachoma, a horrible eye disease which leads to blindness, affects more than half of Egypt's 20 million people. In 1947, some 157 million Asiatics were attacked by filariasis, a horribly debilitating disease.

We would not underrate the great developments made in medical research in past decades in conquering some plagues and diseases. It is very possible that there will yet be great desolations in the form of plagues and diseases. The foregoing data suggest these two things:

(a) New diseases seem to appear from time to time. Our generation knows of some of these, some of which appear to be associated with our civilization in the West.

(b) This generation is afflicted with "mass" diseases that afflict millions of people. Therefore, is it true today that "plagues" and "desolating sickness,"

---

[32]*United Nations World*, "Why the World Is Sick," p. 33.

regardless of what has been in the past, are characteristic of our times, as the Lord declared they would be?

Other Signs

In addition, the destruction of the "great and abominable church," or the church of the devil, is prophesied.[33] This may be interpreted to mean all error, Christian or non-Christian.[34] The voice of the waves of the sea heaving themselves beyond their bounds"[35] and the destructiveness of the waters in the last days,[36] are also signs. An example of this is the storm, caused by tidal waves, which struck Holland, Belgium, and England in February, 1953. Newspaper dispatches report this as the worst storm Europe has experienced in 500 years. Predictions that the Lamanites are to "blossom as the rose," and Jacob (latter-day Israel) is to "rejoice upon the mountains,"[37] are probably in the process of fulfilment.

Effect of Latter-day Conditions

What will be the effect or results of the conditions which will prevail in the last days? The modern revelations speak of famine;[38] "weeping and wailing";[39] "men's hearts shall fail them" and "fear shall come

----

[33]Doc. & Cov. 29:21; 88:94.
[34]I Nephi 13:26-28; 14:8-17; Rev. chaps 17 and 18.
[35]Doc. & Cov. 88:90.
[36]*Ibid.*, 61:5, 14-17.
[37]*Ibid.*, 49:24, 25.
[38]*Ibid.*, 29:16; also Matt. 24:29.
[39]Doc. & Cov. 29:14.

upon all people,"[40] and the gospel will be taken from the Gentiles.[41]

Supplementary Reading: Joseph Fielding Smith, *Signs of the Times*.

---

[40]*Ibid.*, 45:26; 88:91.
[41]*Ibid.*, 45:25; 29, 30.

CHAPTER THREE

"THIS IS A DAY OF WARNING"

(Doc. & Cov. 63:58)

The coming of the Son of Man never will be—never can be till the judgments spoken of for his hour are poured out: which judgments are commenced. (Joseph Fielding Smith, *Teachings of the Prophet Joseph Smith,* p. 286.)

The hour spoken of was prophesied by John the Revelator as "the hour of his (God's) judgment."[1]

Of the nearness of the Lord's coming, the Prophet Joseph Smith wrote:

I will prophesy that the signs of the coming of the Son of Man are already commenced. One pestilence will desolate after another. We shall soon have war and bloodshed. The moon will be turned into blood. I testify of these things, and that the coming of the Son of Man is nigh, even at your doors. (*Ibid.,* p. 160.)

When Joseph Smith uttered these works, he was discharging his divine responsibility as a prophet in calling upon the world to repent. The introductory chapter in this series has provided the reader with a background of material on what the Lord has said about the Prophet Joseph Smith's divine calling and the purpose of the message of this dispensation. In addition, tutorship by angelic personages prepared him for this great calling.

---

[1]Rev. 14:7.

A message of warning was reiterated again and again that the missionaries and members of the Church would understand the need to warn their fellow men.[2] The Lord's servants were sent out under this commission.

> Lift up your voices and spare not. Call upon the nations to repent, both old and young, both bond and free, saying: Prepare yourselves for the great day of the Lord. (Doc. & Cov., 43:20; also 133:8-10.)

But the warning message by His servants will be rejected,[3] although accompanied by famine, pestilences, and other judgments.[4] The instruments of destruction will be poured out, "after your testimony,"[5] "when the cup of their (the nations) iniquity is full."[6] In these words the Lord has given us to understand that we are living in that generation:

> Behold the day has come, when the cup of the wrath of mine indignation is full.
>
> Behold, verily I say unto you, that these are the words of the Lord your God.
>
> Wherefore, labor ye, labor ye in my vineyard for the last time—for the last time call upon the inhabitants of the earth.
>
> For in mine own due time will I come upon the earth in judgment, and my people shall be redeemed and shall reign with me on earth. (*Ibid.*, 43:26-29.)

---

[2] Doc. & Cov. 63:37; 88:81, 82; 133:37-40; 84:96, 97.
[3] *Ibid.*, 45:29.
[4] *Ibid.*, 43:25.
[5] *Ibid.*, 88:88-91.
[6] *Ibid.*, 101:11.

WAR AS A SIGN

One of the signs of the last days which has already demonstrated the divine calling of Joseph Smith as a prophet of God is that of war. This sign is one which, in the opinion of the writer, gives more concrete evidence that we are in the last days than the other signs indicated in the last chapter. This is believed because when war exists it is known by all. Rumors of wars mentioned as another sign of this period are given wide publicity. The terribleness of war, and today its possible involvement of the entire world, have made it number one reading matter.

Within a year after organization of the Church of Jesus Christ of Latter-day Saints, the Lord informed his prophet that although reports of disturbance and wars in far countries were prevalent, "ye know not the hearts of men in your own land."[7] Shortly thereafter, the first indication of the coming of Civil War in the United States was given in these words:

> Ye hear of wars in foreign lands; but, behold I say unto you, they are nigh, even at your doors, and not many years hence ye shall hear of wars in your own lands. (*Ibid.*, 45:63.)

The fact that war was to be even more frequent and universal than confined to a few trouble spots in the world and in the United States, the Lord spoke emphatically. Given in 1831 in a revelation which is the "voice of warning" to the world, the divine mission

---

[7]*Ibid.*, 38:29.

of Joseph Smith, and the purpose and effect of the gospel for the relatively few who would accept it, one finds this significant statement:

> And again, verily I say unto you, O inhabitants of the earth: I the Lord am willing to make these things known unto all flesh;
>
> For I am no respecter of persons, and will that all men shall know that the day speedily cometh; *the hour is not yet, but is nigh at hand, when peace shall be taken from the earth,* and the devil shall have power over his own dominion.
>
> And also the Lord shall have power over his saints and shall reign in their midst, and shall come down in judgment upon Idumea or the world. (*Ibid.,* 1:34-36 Italics author's.)

Although expressed in the future tense, it is clear that peace is to be taken from the earth in this dispensation. Has the time arrived when it can be said that peace has been taken from the earth?

BEGINNING OF WAR IN THE LAST DAYS

The Lord revealed specific information about the conflict between the Southern States and the Northern States, by "a voice,"[8] which is one means of divine communication. In 1832 the Lord revealed that the rebellion of South Carolina would be the beginning of wars in the last days.[8a] But the revelation was not about the Civil War alone, for:

> Verily, thus saith the Lord concerning the wars that will shortly come to pass, beginning at the rebellion of

---

[8]*Ibid.,* 130:12, 13.
[8a]Doc. & Cov. 87:1-2.

South Carolina, which will eventually terminate in the death and misery of many souls;

And the time will come that *war* will be poured out upon all nations, *beginning at this place*. (*Ibid.*, 87:3. Italics author's.)

Military historians have indicated several facts about the American Civil War that verify this truth. Lynn Montress in *War Through the Ages*, writes that the American Civil War as measured by anything in Europe's past was astronomical with statistics. He then proceeds to elaborate upon this point by quoting these facts: (1) more than 2,000 combats took place; (2) 149 of these combats were of such magnitude to classify them as battles; (3) over 500,000 soldiers gave their lives; (4) the cost of the war was astronomical with every resource of the South being used before surrendering to the North.

Other writers, such as J. F. C. Fuller, have emphasized the development of weapons and military tactics in the Civil War that were employed in subsequent wars.[8b]

When Great Britain was to "call upon other nations in order to defend themselves against other nations" we have, in prophecy, a description of World War I, for "then war shall be poured out upon all nations."[9]

[8b]Roy W. Doxey, *Prophecies and Prophetic Promises from the Doctrine and Covenants*, p. 192.
[9]*Ibid.*, 87:3.

EVENTS FUTURE

In preserving the order of events given in the remainder of this prophecy, one might well believe that the events are yet future. This would, however, allow for the partial fulfillment of some of these events in the past, as for example, "slaves shall rise up against their masters who shall be marshaled and disciplined for war,"[10] as Negro soldiers were during the Civil War. But are there not slaves in the world today (people in bondage without the freedom to act because of unrighteous leaders) who may yet rise up against their masters? The "remnants who are left of the land will marshal themselves"[11] may not only be the American Indians in the Indian wars, but also the many millions of natives on this continent.

President Daniel H. Wells, counselor to President Brigham Young, taught that the remnant spoken of in this prophecy was the Indian who would one day vex the gentile nation, the United States, with a sore vexation.[11a]

The extent of the tribulation in the last days is cogently expressed in this verse:

> And thus, with the sword and by bloodshed the inhabitants of the earth shall mourn; and with famine, and plague, and earthquake, and the thunder of heaven, and the fierce and vivid lightning also, shall the in-

---

[10]*Ibid.*, 87:4.
[11]*Ibid.*, 87:5.
[11a]Roy W. Doxey, *Prophecies and Prophetic Promises from the Doctrine and Covenants*, p. 197.

habitants of the earth be made to feel the wrath, and indignation, and chastening hand of an Almighty God, until the consumption decreed hath made a full end of all nations. (Doc. & Cov. 87:6.)

From this great revelation on wars, is there not further confirmation that there will be a time when peace is taken from the earth and Satan shall have power over his own dominion?[12] That time is to be in this dispensation of the gospel as we draw nearer to the second coming of Christ, when the judgments will have prepared the way for "a full end of all nations." This will allow for the removal of wickedness from the earth and the reign of Jesus Christ as King of kings and Lord of lords.

Every Latter-day Saint should ask himself this question, "Has peace been taken from the earth?"

WHEAT AND TARES

Because of the importance of the parable known as the wheat and the tares[13] as it applies to the last days, the Master has given further information about it in our dispensation. Aside from slight differences from the New Testament version, as given in verses 1-3 of Section 86 of the Doctrine and Covenants, the following is most pertinent:

But behold, in the last days, even now while the Lord is beginning to bring forth the word, and the blade is springing up and is yet tender—

---

[12]*Ibid.*, 1:34-36.
[13]Matt. 13:24-30, 36-43.

> Behold, verily I say unto you, the angels are crying unto the Lord day and night, who are ready and wait- to be sent forth to reap down the fields;
>
> But the Lord saith unto them, pluck not up the tares while the blade is yet tender (for verily your faith is weak), lest you destroy the wheat also.
>
> Therefore, let the wheat and the tares grow together until the harvest is fully ripe; then ye shall first gather out the wheat from among the tares and after the gathering of the wheat, behold and lo, the tares are bound in bundles, and the field remaineth to be burned. (*Ibid.*, 86:4-7).

By vision, President Wilford Woodruff was permitted to see the judgments of the last days. At a testimony meeting of Salt Lake temple workers in Brigham City, Utah, June 24, 1894, he gave this inspired instruction. His remarks were given under "the power and influence of the Holy Ghost on this occasion, so much so that it not only thrilled his own voice, but shook the hearts of his hearers." Note the reference to "the angels of destruction" and the "wheat and the tares."

> I want to ask this congregation a question: When I have the vision of the night opened continually before my eyes, and can see the mighty judgments that are about to be poured out upon this world, when I know these things are true, and are at the door of Jew and Gentile; while I know I am holding this position before God and this world, can I withhold my voice from lifting up a warning to this people and to the nations of the earth? I may never meet with this people again; I cannot tell how that may be. But while I live and see these things continually before my eyes I shall

raise my warning voice. Now the question I wanted
to ask you is this: We have fourteen million people[13a] on
this earth, and over them all there hangs a cloud of
darkness almost entirely upon their shoulders. Can you
tell me where the people are who will be shielded and
protected from these great calamities and judgments
which are even now at our doors? I'll tell you. The
priesthood of God who honor their priesthood, and
who are worthy of their blessings, are the only ones
who shall have this safety and protection. They are the
only mortal beings. No other people have the right to
be shielded from these judgments. They are at our very
doors; not even this people will escape them entirely.
They will come down like the judgments of Sodom and
Gomorrah. And none but the priesthood will be safe
from their fury. God has held the angels of destruction for many years, lest they should reap down the
wheat with the tares. But I want to tell you now, that
those angels have left the portals of heaven, and they
stand over this people and this nation now, and are
hovering over the earth waiting to pour out the judgments. And from this very day they shall be poured
out. Calamities and troubles are increasing in the
earth, and there is a meaning to these things. Remem-
ber this, and reflect upon these matters. If you do
your duty, and I do my duty, we'll have protection,
and shall pass through the affliction in peace and
safety. Read the scriptures and the revelations. They
will tell you about all these things. Great changes are
at our doors. The next twenty years will see mighty
changes among the nations of the earth. You will live
to see these things, whether I do or not. I have felt
oppressed with the weight of these matters, and I felt

[13a]This is an obvious typographical error, for there were between 1,400
and 1,500 million people on the earth in 1890.

I must speak of them here. It's by the power of the gospel that we shall escape. (*The Young Woman's Journal*, Vol. 5, pp. 512-513.)

The prophetic element in these words has already been verified in the fact that twenty years later (1914) World War I broke out in fury upon the nations. The area covered, destruction wrought, and lives lost had never before been equaled in modern history.

HAS WAR CEASED?

Has actual warfare ceased in the world since the beginning of the first world war? From 1918 to the beginning of World War II in 1939, when Germany invaded Poland, war has not ceased in the world. In an Associated Press dispatch reporting the ten best news items during the year 1945, this comment was made under the title "Postwar Upheavals Again, 1946 Preview":

> When the armistice was signed on Nov. 11, 1918, bringing to a conclusion the first world conflict, the peace was hailed everywhere as the end of wars forever. A statistician later made a check and came to the conclusion that some conflict or other was in progress some place in the world right down to the outbreak of World War II. The story is much the same today. There are still sore spots in Europe; Java is in revolt, the situation in Indo-China is obscure. China is in ferment, India is unsatisfied, and the Arab world is astir over Palestine. The picture is clouded. (*The Evening Bulletin*, Philadelphia, Pa., December 28 (AP), 1945.)

The condition of continuous unrest and warfare had done something to the people of the world during the 1918-1939 period. This is well stated by the historian Thomas A. Bailey of Stanford University, who, in contrasting the war that came in 1914 with the one begun in 1939, wrote:

> By 1939, the world was calloused to an all-out war. The Shanghai shambles of 1932 and 1937, the Ethiopian massacres in 1936, the Barcelonian butcheries of 1938 had all conditioned public opinion. The wiping out of civilian centers had come to be recognized as a new development in the art of "civilized" warfare. Otherwise, the American people, shocked into a defense of outraged humanity, might have entered the war much sooner than they did. (*A Diplomatic History of the American People*, 3d ed., p. 756.)

The magnitude of the second world war far eclipsed in area covered, and lives lost, that of the war begun in 1914. The atomic bomb and other recent instruments of warfare outpowered in destructiveness other wars.

What about the upheavals of World War II enumerated in the newspaper items of 1945? Has war ceased? Relying on memory alone, each one of us could answer this question in the negative. Sore spots in the world have inflamed into war. Despite peace efforts (1953), the world is drawn into two camps, and preparation for another and even more destructive world war goes on. The invasion of South Korea by North Korea in June, 1950, under Communist leadership which brought the United States directly into the war, has called this forcibly to the attention of Americans.

Just two months before the Korean War, President George Albert Smith, in general conference, said this:

> It will not be long until calamities will overtake the human family unless there is speedy repentance. It will not be long before those who are scattered over the face of the earth by millions will die like flies because of what will come. (*Conference Report*, 120th Annual Conference, April, 1950, p. 169.)

PEACE HAS BEEN TAKEN FROM THE EARTH

The Lord has said by His modern Prophets that war and other judgments would be poured out upon the nations and that these are at our doors. In 1831 He revealed that "peace shall be taken from the earth" in this dispensation. For 40 years there has been "some conflict or other" in progress some place in the world. This includes two world wars. In view of these things, is there a Latter-day Saint who cannot agree with this statement: *Peace has been taken from the earth?* In the next chapter we shall say something of war predicted to occur in the future.

REWARDS OF LIVING THE GOSPEL

In this and the last chapter, our attention has been directed to signs of the last days. These constitute a warning message to the world that the way of escape from the predicted judgments is by repentance. President George Albert Smith warned the world that "the price of peace is righteousness." To members of the Church the rewards of living the gospel were stated over a hundred years ago:

> But learn that he who doeth the works of righteousness shall receive his reward, even peace in this world, and eternal life in the world to come. (Doc. & Cov. 59:23.)

The purpose of the signs of the times for members of the Church is to assist them to live worthily, that these blessings may come to them. We should ask ourselves this question: Do we love the Lord sufficiently that we will keep His commandments, even to the point of "looking forth for the signs of his coming?"[14] On the other hand, shall we place ourselves in the position of the early members of the Church about whom the Lord said that in the day of their peace they esteemed lightly His counsel, and therefore in the time of their trouble He was slow to hearken unto their prayers?[15]

---

[14]Doc. & Cov. 45:39.
[15]*Ibid.*, 101:7, 8.

CHAPTER FOUR

THE SECOND COMING OF CHRIST

Elder Joseph Fielding Smith, President of the Quorum of the Twelve, in the April general conference of 1951, said of the nearness of the Lord's coming:

> I believe that the coming of the Son of God is not far away, how far I do not know, but I do know that it is over one hundred years nearer than it was when Elijah the prophet came to the Prophet Joseph Smith and Oliver Cowdery in the Kirtland Temple on the third day of April, 1836. Elijah's words point to the fact that we are that much nearer. And this ancient prophet declared that by the restoration of those keys we should know that the great and dreadful day of the Lord is near, even at our doors. (*Conference Report*, 121st Annual Conference, April, 1951, p. 58.)

The leaders of the Church of Jesus Christ of Latter-day Saints from the Prophet Joseph Smith to the present have not attempted to tell the world when the second coming of Christ would be. But they have lifted up a warning voice that His coming is to be in this dispensation, which began in the spring of 1820. That the Lord's coming in power and glory is nearer is clearly evident to all, as stated by President Smith.

THE SIGN OF THE SON OF MAN

As Latter-day Saints, we can expect to be informed by the Prophet of the Lord of the appearance of the

"Sign of the Son of Man," mentioned by Jesus to His disciples in the Meridian of Time[1] and spoken of again in this dispensation as "a great sign in heaven, and all people shall see it together."[2] What is this sign? Because all people shall see it, does it follow that it will be recognized by the world as a sign indicating that the Lord's coming is near, or will it be explained as another natural phenomenon? The answer to the first question has not been revealed. Inasmuch as wickness and unbelief will reign on the earth near the Lord's coming the world will not accept this great sign for what it is.

In February, 1843, the Prophet Joseph Smith reported that a Mr. Redding had claimed he saw the sign of the Son of Man. In commenting up this, the Prophet said: "He has not seen the sign of the Son of Man as foretold by Jesus; neither has any man, nor will any man, until after the sun shall have been darkened and the moon bathed in blood: for the Lord hath not shown me any such signs; and as the prophet saith, so it must be—"Surely the Lord God will do nothing, but he revealeth his secret unto his servants the prophets." (See Amos 3:7.)[3]

> There will be wars and rumors of wars, signs in the heavens above and on the earth beneath, the sun turned into darkness and the moon to blood, earthquakes in divers places, the seas heaving beyond their bounds; then will appear one grand sign of the Son of Man in

---

[1]Matt. 24:36; Luke 21:25-27.
[2]Doc. & Cov. 88:93.
[3]*The Teachings of the Prophet Joseph Smith*, p. 280.

heaven. But what will the world do? They will say it is
a planet, a comet, etc. But the Son of Man will come as
the sign of the coming of the Son of Man, which will
be as the light of the morning cometh out of the east.
(*The Teachings of the Prophet Joseph Smith*, p. 286-7.)

NOT ONE BUT MANY SIGNS

It is well to keep in mind that there is no one sign
or event which signalizes the nearness of the Lord's
coming. All of the signs together mark our period
as being the last days. The momentum of occurrence
of these signs of the times has greatly increased. Events
yet future may follow one after another in rapid succession. It should be apparent that one of these signs—
the removal of peace from the earth—is a reality. That
this will continue either as armed conflict (the pattern
for many years now), or as preparation for war seems
apparent. In the *Age of Conflict* the authors express
this fact by suggesting that since 1914, the beginning
of World War I, intervening wars and crises are but
episodes in a single Age of Conflict, but it has not run
its course.[3a] The Lord has said in this regard:

> For behold, and lo, vengeance cometh speedily upon
> the ungodly as the whirlwind; and who shall escape it?
> The Lord's scourge shall pass over by night and by
> day, and the report thereof shall vex all people: yea,
> *it shall not be stayed until the Lord come;*
> For the indignation of the Lord is kindled against
> their abominations and all their wicked works. (Doc.
> & Cov. 97:22-24. Italics author's.)

[3a]Roy W. Doxey, *Prophecies and Prophetic Promises from the Doctrine
and Covenants,* p. 198.

In the path of war, famine has stalked the land. It has come without war. The world is yet to see more of this as a sign of the last days. Of this the Prophet Joseph Smith said:

> I have asked of the Lord concerning His coming; and while asking the Lord, He gave a sign and said, "In the days of Noah I set a bow in the heavens as a sign and token that in any year that the bow should be seen the Lord would not come; but there should be seed time and harvest during that year; but whenever you see the bow withdrawn, it shall be a token that there shall be famine, pestilence, and great distress among the nations, and that the coming of the Messiah is not far distant. (*History of the Church* 6:254.)

Latter-day Saints have been counseled to be prepared for this and any other emergency which might arise by following counsel in Church welfare matters. When President David O. McKay dedicated the granary on Welfare Square (Salt Lake City), he said in that dedicatory prayer:

> May this be an edifice of service, a contribution of love, and as such we dedicate it to thee and ask thy blessings to attend all who may have contributed to its erection, and all who may contribute to the keeping of these bins filled with wheat *which is considered necessary to be preserved preparatory for the judgments that await the nations of the earth.* (David O. McKay, August 1, 1940, quoted by Elder Harold B. Lee, 113th Annual Conference, *Conference Report,* April, 1943, p. 126.)

BE PREPARED

During His mortal ministry the Lord spoke directly to the preparedness of believers in the last days. The

parable of the Ten Virgins,[4] five of whom were prepared to meet the Bridegroom, while the remaining
five were unprepared and rejected from entrance to
the marriage feast, is closed with this application:
"Verily I say unto you, I know you not.

"Watch therefore, for ye know neither the day nor
the hour wherein the Son of man cometh."[5]

In our generation the Lord has referred to this
parable and its application to His second coming.

> These things are the things that ye must look for;
> and, speaking after the manner of the Lord, they are
> now nigh at hand, and in a time to come, even in the
> day of the coming of the Son of Man.
>
> And until that hour there will be foolish virgins
> among the wise; and at that hour cometh an entire
> separation of the righteous and the wicked; and in that
> day will I send mine angels to pluck out the wicked and
> cast them into unquenchable fire. (Doc. & Cov. 63:53-
> 54.)
>
> And at that day, when I shall come in my glory,
> shall the parable be fulfilled which I spake concerning
> the ten virgins.
>
> For they that are wise and have received the truth,
> and have taken the Holy Spirit for their guide, and
> have not been deceived—verily, I say unto you, they
> shall not be hewn down and cast into the fire, but shall
> abide the day.
>
> And the earth shall be given unto them for an in-
> heritance; and they shall multiply and wax strong, and
> their children shall grow up without sin unto salvation.

---

[4]Matt. 25:1-13.
[5]For full explanation consult James E. Talmage, *Jesus the Christ*, pp.
576-580.

> For the Lord shall be in their midst, and his glory shall be upon them, and he will be their king and their lawgiver. (Doc. & Cov. 45:56-59.)

It is significant that in this parable the virgins are those who profess belief in Jesus Christ and are members of His Church. Some are "foolish virgins among the wise."[5a] Those of the Church who are prepared for His coming shall inherit the earth as their permanent abode in fellowship with the Father and the Son.[6]

The exact date when the Savior shall come in power and glory is unknown.[7] The Lord has said, however, that He will come when the world does not expect Him.[8] There will be those who will say "that Christ delayeth his coming, until the end of the earth."[9] The second coming of Christ as a real event is not considered seriously by many Christians.

As indicated in this and preceding chapters this doctrine has been an important part of the message of the Dispensation of the Fulness of Times. Yet notwithstanding this, there are probably many Latter-day Saints who have not considered what the Lord has said about it.

PEOPLE CLASSIFIED

One of the most informative articles upon this subject was written by President Charles W. Penrose

----

5aDoc. & Cov. 63:54; Harold B. Lee, *Conference Report,* October, 1951, pp. 26-27.
6Doc. & Cov. 76:62; 88:17-20.
7Matt. 24:40; Doc. & Cov. 49:7.
8Matt. 24:41-53; Doc. & Cov. 61:38.
9*Ibid.,* 45:26.

for the *Millennial Star,* September 10, 1859. His views
are also in accord with what the Prophet Joseph Smith
wrote.[10] The inhabitants of the earth at the time immediately preceding the coming of Christ may be
considered under three general divisions, wrote President Penrose.

> First, the Saints of God gathered to one place on
> the Western continent called Zion, busily preparing for
> His appearance in their midst as their Redeemer, who
> had shed His blood for their salvation, now coming to
> reign over them and to reward them for their labors
> in establishing His government:
>
> Second, the Jews gathered to Jerusalem and also
> expecting the Messiah, but not believing that Jesus of
> Nazareth was the Son of God, and being in danger
> of destruction from their Gentile enemies:
>
> Third, the corrupt nations and kingdoms of men,
> who, rejecting the light of the Gospel are unprepared
> for the Lord's advent and are almost ripe for destruc-
> tion. (*Liahona,* 21:397.)

THE APPEARANCES OF THE SAVIOR

To each one of these classes the Lord will appear,
and in the order mentioned. Accordingly, one might
consider the second coming of Jesus as being made
up of three appearances. The time interval between
these appearances is not indicated in the scriptures.
It is evident that the second and third are very close
together and might be considered as one. Almost
without exception, however, the scriptures refer to

---

[10]*History of the Church,* 4:610.

the last appearance as His coming, because of the greater display of power when the wicked are destroyed from the earth.

In a modern revelation the Lord has declared that His coming will be vastly different from His first appearance among men at birth. Because missionaries were to go among a religious sect known as the Shaking Quakers or Reform Quakers, who believed that their leader, a woman, was Jesus Christ incarnate, this information was given:

> And again, verily I say unto you, that the Son of Man cometh not in the form of a woman, neither of a man traveling on the earth.
>
> Wherefore, be not deceived but continuing in steadfastness, looking forth for the heavens to be shaken, and the earth to tremble and to reel to and fro as a drunken man, and for the valleys to be exalted, and for the mountains to be made low, and for the rough places to become smooth—and all this when the angel shall sound his trumpet. . . .
>
> Behold, I am Jesus Christ, and I come quickly. (Doc. & Cov. 49:22-23, 28.)

PLACE OF REFUGE

The Lord has set forth in ancient and modern times that there would be two gathering places in the last days—Palestine and America.[11]

The Mount Zion of the latter days is the city of the New Jerusalem to be built upon the American

---

[11]Micah 4:1, 2; Doc. & Cov. 133:12, 13.

continent in the state of Missouri.[12] In this place the temple of the Lord will be built as prophesied.[13]

The gathering of the Saints to Zion in this dispensation is to establish it as "a refuge from the storm, and from wrath when it shall be poured out without mixture upon the whole earth."[14] The New Jerusalem is designated as "a land of peace, a city of refuge, a place of safety for the saints of the Most High God."[15]

In the troublous days of the wars of the last days, Zion will be the "only people that shall not be at war one with another," but "the glory of the Lord shall be there, and the terror of the Lord also shall be there."[16]

THE FIRST APPEARANCE—TO THE SAINTS

The Lord's first appearance as part of the second coming will be to his Saints. Of such an appearance the Old Testament prophet spoke when he referred to the Lord's suddenly coming to His temple in the day when it could be appropriately asked: "But who may abide the day of his coming? and who shall stand when he appeareth? for he is like a refiner's fire, and like fuller's soap."[17] Moroni quoted part of this chapter to Joseph Smith when he visited him in 1823.[18]

---

[12]Doc. & Cov. 84:2, 3; Ether 13:4-6.
[13]*Ibid.*, 84:4, 5.
[14]*Ibid.*, 115:6.
[15]*Ibid.*, 45:66.
[16]*Ibid.*, 45:67-71.
[17]Malachi 3:2.
[18]Pearl of Great Price, Jos. Smith 2:36.

It may be concluded that this appearance to the Saints may not be generally known except as the world is informed of it by the Saints. A partial fulfilment of this prophecy was the appearance of the Savior in the Kirtland Temple in 1836.[19] President Wilford Woodruff recalled a prophecy made by Joseph Smith in 1832, ten years before the prediction that the saints would go to the Rocky Mountains as follows:

> It will fill the Rocky Mountains. There will be tens of thousands of Latter-day Saints who will be gathered to the Rocky Mountains, and there they will open the door for the establishing of the gospel among the Lamanites, who will receive the gospel and their endowments and the blessings of God. This people will go into the Rocky Mountains; they will there build temples to the Most High. They will raise up a posterity there, and the Latter-day Saints who dwell in these mountains will stand in the flesh until the coming of the Son of Man. The Son of Man will come to them while in the Rocky Mountains.
>
> I name these things because I want to bear testimony before God, angels, and men that mine eyes behold the day, and have beheld for the last fifty years of my life, the fulfilment of that prophecy. I never expected to see the Rocky Mountains when I listened to that man's voice, but I have, and do today. I will say here that I shall not live to see it, you may not live to see it; but these thousands of Latter-day Saint children that belong to the Sabbath schools, I believe many of them will stand in the flesh when the Lord Jesus Christ visits the Zion of God here in the mountains of Israel. (*Conference Report,* April 1898.)

---

[19]Doc. & Cov. 110:1-4.

That the complete fulfilment has reference to the temple in the New Jerusalem is indicated by reason of the offering to be made by the sons of Levi.[20] President Brigham Young said that "when Jesus makes his next appearance upon the earth, but few of this Church will be prepared to receive him and see him face to face and converse with him; but he will come to his temple."[21]

Some of the Saints by appointment will attend the great council at Adam-ondi-Ahman[22] spoken of by the Prophet Joseph Smith. At that time Adam delivers up his stewardship to Christ preparatory to "the coming of the Son of Man" in glory.[23]

SECOND APPEARANCE—TO THE JEWS

The next great appearance of the Master will be at a time when the Jews are gathered to the Holy Land. When this happens the nations will be at war with the Jews, who since 1948 have had their own government in Israel (Palestine), to which the Jews are now gathering. The Prophet declares that when sorely besieged and part of Jerusalem is taken,[24] two prophets or witnesses "raised up to the Jewish nation in the last days" will be killed and their dead bodies shall lie in

---

[20]Malachi 3:3; Doc. & Cov. 84:21-34; *Teachings of the Prophet Joseph Smith*, p. 171-3.
[21]John A. Widtsoe, *Discourses of Brigham Young*, p. 176.
[22]Doc. & Cov. 116.
[23]*Teachings of the Prophet Joseph Smith*, p. 157; for a full discussion see Joseph Fielding Smith, *The Way to Perfection*, ch. 40.
[24]Zechariah 14:1, 2.

the streets three days and a half. Life will re-enter their bodies, which will ascend into heaven. A great earthquake will cause the Mount of Olives to divide and the earth will tremble.[25] The Lord will then fight their battle.[26] At this time they will ask, "What are these wounds in thine hands and in thy feet?"

> Then shall they know that I am the Lord; for I will say unto them: These wounds are the wounds with which I was wounded in the house of my friends. I am he who was lifted up. I am Jesus that was crucified. I am the Son of God. (Doc. & Cov. 45:51, 52; Zechariah 13:6.)
>
> And then shall they weep because of their iniquities; then shall they lament because they persecuted their king. (Doc. & Cov. 45:53; Zechariah 12:8-14, 13:1.)

And thus Judah shall be redeemed by acceptance of the Savior of all mankind through obedience to the fulness of the gospel.[26a] Confirmatory of these appearances, President Brigham Young said:

> We have a great desire for their welfare, and are looking for the time soon to come when they will gather to Jerusalem, build up the city and the land of Palestine, and prepare for the coming of the Messiah. When he comes again he will not come as he did when the Jews rejected him; neither will he appear first at Jerusalem when he makes his second appearance on the earth; but he will appear first on the land where he commenced his work in the beginning, and planted the garden of Eden, and that was done in the land of America.

---

[25]Revelation 11:1-13; Doc. & Cov. 77:15; 45:48-50.
[26]Zechariah 14:3-9.
[26a]Doc. & Cov. 133:35.

When the Savior visits Jerusalem, and the Jews look upon him, and see the wounds in his hands and in his side and in his feet, they will then know that they have persecuted and put to death the true Messiah, and then they will acknowledge him, but not till then. They have confounded his first and second coming, expecting his first coming to be as a mighty prince instead of as a servant. They will go back by and by to Jerusalem and own their Lord and Master. We have no feelings against them. (Brigham Young, *Journal of Discourses* 11:279.)

THIRD APPEARANCE—IN POWER TO THE WORLD

There follows the great and glorious coming of Jesus Christ, who subdues all enemies under his feet, "and the Lord shall be king over all the earth." This is the coming for which the righteous have prayed, that wickedness might be removed from the earth. His coming in power is described in the modern revelation as "an entire separation of the righteous and the wicked,"[27] with the wicked being consumed.[28] The nations of the earth will be afraid, for the Lord "shall be terrible unto them, that fear may seize upon them."[29]

And prepare for the revelation which is to come, when the veil of the covering of my temple, in my tabernacle, which hideth the earth, shall be taken off, and all flesh shall see me together.

And every corruptible thing, both of man, or of the beasts of the field, or of the fowls of the heavens,

---

[27]Doc. & Cov. 63:54.
[28]*Ibid.*, 63:34.
[29]*Ibid.*, 45:74, 75; 34: 7, 8.

or of the fish of the sea, that dwells upon all the face
of the earth, shall be consumed. (Doc. & Cov. 101:23-
24; Cf. 133:63-64.)

The scriptures also tell of other great events to
take place when the Lord comes. These events, such
as the resurrection, the Saints who are alive being
caught up to meet the Savior, and so forth, will be
considered in subsequent chapters.

Thus the earth will be prepared to enter into its
next phase of existence—the millennium of peace and
righteousness.

CHAPTER FIVE

THE MILLENNIUM

The transition from a period of destruction when great judgments befall the inhabitants of the earth, as discussed in previous chapters, and a period of peace and righteousness oftimes raises many problems in the minds of Latter-day Saints. Such questions as these are common: If these judgments come to the people of the earth, does that mean it is the end of the world? Will the Latter-day Saints who are scattered in the nations be safe, or will they be asked to gather to Zion? Will everyone be immortal or resurrected, as some have interpreted the scriptures which say that the Saints on the earth will be caught up to meet the Savior,[1] or will there be mortal beings on the earth during the millenium?

THE END OF THE WORLD

The Master was asked by his disciples of "the sign of thy coming, and of the end of the world."[2] Later in the same discussion the Lord said the gospel "shall be preached in all the world for a witness unto all nations; and then shall the end come."[3] Without further clarification, people have understood this to mean the end of all, or the end of the earth. By in-

---

[1] I Thessalonians 4:16-18; Doc. & Cov. 88:96.
[2] Matthew 24:3.
[3] *Ibid.*, 24:14.

spiration of the Lord to the Prophet Joseph we learn that Jesus defined these expressions—"end of the world" and "then shall the end come"—as "the destruction of the wicked."[4] Previous chapters have dealt with this destruction. What of the righteous members of The Church of Jesus Christ of Latter-day Saints? Are Latter-day Saints the only ones who shall not be destroyed?

Stand in Holy Places

Unto the Book of Mormon Prophet Nephi, the Lord revealed that in our day the faithful Saints would enjoy the power of God though "scattered upon all the face of the earth; and they were armed with righteousness and with the power of God in great glory."[5] These Saints are commanded to "stand in holy places"[6] and the Lord would designate places of gathering for them.[7] That this responsibility rests upon the divinely appointed leaders of this dispensation has been stated by Elder Harold B. Lee, of the First Presidency:

> Thus, clearly the Lord has placed the responsibility for directing the work of gathering in the hands of the leaders of the Church to whom he will reveal his will where and when such gatherings would take place in the future. It would be well—before the frightening event concerning the fulfillment of all God's promises and predictions are upon us, that the Saints in every

---

[4]P. of G. P., Joseph Smith 1:4, 31.
[5]I Nephi 14:14.
[6]Doc. & Cov. 101:22.
[7]Doc. & Cov. 101:20.

land prepare themselves and look forward to the instruction that shall come to them from the First Presidency of this Church as to where they shall be gathered
and not be disturbed in their feelings until such instruction is given to them as it is revealed by the Lord
to the proper authority. (*Conference Report*, 118th
Annual Conference, April, 1948, p. 55.)

Is it to be expected that in the days of trouble, all
Latter-day Saints will be preserved from disease, war,
and other judgments? The Prophet Joseph Smith spoke
of this question as follows:

I explained concerning the coming of the Son of
Man; also that it is a false idea that the Saints will escape all the judgements, whilst the wicked suffer; for all
flesh is subject to suffer, and "the righteous shall hardly
escape"; still many of the Saints will escape for the just
shall live by faith; yet many of the righteous shall fall
prey to disease, to pestilence, etc., by reason of the
weakness of the flesh, and yet be saved in the kingdom
of God.   So that it is an unhallowed principle to say
that such and such have transgressed because they have
been preyed upon by disease or death, for all flesh is
subject to death; and the Savior has said, "Judge not,
lest ye be judged." (*Teachings of the Prophet Joseph
Smith*, p. 162-3.)

THE SAINTS ONLY?

Let us now ask ourselves, "Are there to be other
people on the earth than Latter-day Saints following
the second coming of Christ?"

In the Tenth Article of Faith, Latter-day Saints
profess belief in the return of the Ten Tribes from

the land of the north. Although the scriptures are not explicit as to the time when they shall return, it would appear to be at or near the second coming of Christ. The Prophet Joseph Smith taught that war, pestilence, hail, famine, and earthquake would destroy the wicked and "prepare the way for the return of the lost tribes from the north country."[8] Following a description of the universal appearance of the Lord at His coming, even that "his voice shall be heard among all people," the return of the lost tribes is described. They shall come to the children of Ephraim (Latter-day Saints) and there receive their blessings.[9]

Inasmuch as the scriptures speak of only the destruction of the wicked or unrighteous as a class, one can believe that the honorable and just who are not members of The Church of Jesus Christ of Latter-day Saints are prepared to live on the earth during the millennium.[9a] From what the Lord has given concerning the salvation of this group, those whose lives are in accord with terrestrial law,[10] further confirmation of this fact is given. Observance of celestial law requires ordinances and faithfulness to covenants thus made, in addition to a life in accord with the moral teachings of the gospel which is the honorable or terrestrial way of life.

The Lord is also mindful of another class of mankind—those who "knew no law" or the heathen na-

---

[8]*History of the Church* 1:315.
[9]Doc. & Cov. 133:26-34; III Nephi 21:26; Ether 13:11.
[9a]Joseph Fielding Smith, *The Way to Perfection,* p. 312.
[10]Doc. & Cov. 76:73-77.

tions.[11] These will enjoy the blessings of the millennium. If among these nations there are those, however, who will not come up to worship, they will suffer "the judgments of God and must eventually be destroyed from the earth."[12] This is in accord with what the Prophet Zechariah said of the nations who were left of those who came up to fight against Jerusalem.[13]

It necessarily follows that after the second coming of Christ there will be mortal beings upon the earth. In a number of places in the scriptures reference is made to the Saints being caught up to meet the Savior when He comes,[14] and also that the resurrection of the righteous will take place.[15] It should be understood that the Saints alive at the Savior's coming will continue to live as mortal beings.

> And he that liveth when the Lord shall come, and hath kept the faith, blessed is he; nevertheless, it is appointed to him to die at the age of man. (Doc. & Cov. 63:50.)

LIFE CONTINUES

Children will be born and live to the "age of a tree"[16] as mortal beings, but there shall be no sorrow arising from death.[17] This is because they will not sleep in the dust, "but shall be changed in the twin-

---

[11]*Ibid.*, 45:54.
[12]Joseph Fielding Smith, *Teachings of the Prophet Joseph Smith*, p. 269.
[13]Zechariah 14:16-19.
[14]I Thessalonians 4:16-18; Doc. & Cov. 76:102; 88:96.
[15]I Corinthians 15:23; Doc. & Cov. 88:98, 99.
[16]*Ibid.*, 101:30; Isaiah 65:20.
[17]Doc. & Cov. 101:29.

kling of an eye, and shall be caught up, and his (their) rest shall be glorious."[18] The changing of the body will be from mortality to immortality or resurrection. This is also said of the Three Nephites, who, though not mortal in the same sense but are translated beings, also eventually subject to death, will receive their resurrection at the Savior's coming.[19]

Life during the millennium, ushered in by the appearance of the Lord in great power and glory, will continue. People shall "build houses, and inhabit them; and they shall plant vineyards, and eat the fruit of them" unmolested, for the peoples of the earth shall be at peace "and shall long enjoy the work of their hands."[20]

With Satan bound, that he will not have power to tempt any man,[21] and enmity between all flesh removed,[22] corruption and vice among men will cease. The millennium is a period when the righteous will live on the earth and love will abound.[23]

WICKEDNESS DURING THE MILLENNIUM

In writing to the question, "Will there be any wickedness upon the earth during the millennium?" President Joseph Fielding Smith has given us this instructive information:

It is true that the Lord will come suddenly, for such a coming he has promised, but that all the conditions

---

[18]*Ibid.*, 101:31; 63:51.
[19]III Nephi 28:8.
[20]Isaiah 65:21-23.

[21]Doc. & Cov. 101:28; 43:30, 31.
[22]*Ibid.*, 101:26; Isaiah 65:25; 11:6-9.
[23]Doc. & Cov. 101:27, 35.

and vicissitudes connected with the reign of peace will be ushered in suddenly at the time of his coming would hardly be a reasonable conclusion. The Lord works on natural principles. The preparatory work for the millennial reign is now under way and must continue for some time, I take it, even after He comes. People will have to be taught, the proper instruction will of necessity have to be given, the gospel will have to be declared, and this will take time. Satan is to be bound, as the scriptures say, that he shall have no power to tempt any man, but the traditions of the centuries will still exist and the influence they have on the minds of the children of men will not be removed in a moment. Men have their agency and will be able to act for themselves even after Satan is bound, and the effects of teachings and traditions will remain with them even to the extent that perhaps some will fail to understand the gospel and receive it. However, I take it, these will be very few. When the time comes that "death is removed and man lives to the age of a tree," if he has not received the Gospel he is a sinner and under condemnation and therefore worthy of being cursed. Wickedness and sin as we comprehend the meaning of these expressions now, will *not* prevail during the Millennium. The Lord however calls all men *wicked* who do not receive the fulness of his gospel. (Doc. & Cov. 35:12; 84:49-53.) King Benjamin said—and he was instructed by an angel—"that the blood of Christ atoned for the sins of those who have fallen by the transgression of Adam, who have died not knowing the will of God concerning them, or who have ignorantly sinned" (Mosiah 3:11), but that the time would come —and that time must be during the Millennium—"when the knowledge of a Savior shall spread throughout every nation, kindred, tongue and people. And behold, when *that* time cometh, *none* shall be found blameless before God, *except* it be little children, *only* through repentance and faith on the name of the Lord God Omnipotent." (Verses 20-21.)   Man will still have his agency even after Satan is bound, and will follow his traditions and inclinations to some extent at least, if he shall so choose.   But the nations will be forced to acknowledge the reign of the Great King or punishment shall be meted out to them.   Corruption and vice shall be done away, those who indulge in such practices shall be swept off from the face of the earth, and it shall be as it was in the days of the great Nephite destruction at the time of the crucifixion, that only the more righteous or the better class of mankind, including the heathen, shall be left. (Doc. & Cov. 45:54.) (*Improvement Era*, Vol. 23:1112, 1113, October, 1920.)

INCREASED KNOWLEDGE

Knowledge will greatly increase, for the Lord will reveal all things. In that day answers to questions which have perplexed mankind concerning the creation of the earth and man—"things that are in the earth, and upon the earth, and in heaven"—will be made known.[24] It is probable that during the millennium the sealed part of the Book of Mormon will be revealed, for it "shall not be delivered in the day of wickedness and abominations of the people," but when "all things shall be revealed unto the children of men."[25]

Jesus Christ will reign upon the earth with His Saints for the thousand-year period of peace and

[24]Doc. & Cov. 101:32-34.
[25]II Nephi 27:7, 8, 10, 11, 22.

righteousness.[26] Will He remain and dwell upon the earth a thousand years? Brigham Young said: He will come here, and return to His mansions where He dwells with His Father, and come again to the earth and again return to His Father, according to my understanding."[27] The Prophet Joseph Smith recorded that:

> Christ and the resurrected Saints will reign over the earth during the thousand years. They will not probably dwell upon the earth, but will visit it when they please, or when it is necessary to govern it. (*History of the Church*, 5:212.)

Thus the affairs of the world will be regulated, because the reins of government will be in the Savior's hands and "judgment will be administered in righteousness; anarchy and confusion will be destroyed, and 'nations will learn war no more'."[28]

GREAT CHANGES ON THE EARTH

When the Lord comes to reign, great changes will occur on the earth. Terrestrial conditions will prevail, and the land will return to its former place before its division in the patriarchal dispensation.[29] This renewal of the earth is considered to be paradisiacal glory mentioned in the Tenth Article of Faith.[30] This is the condition of rest which shall come to the earth.[31]

---

[26]Revelation 20:6; Doc. & Cov. 133:25.
[27]*Discourses of Brigham Young*, p. 176.
[28]*History of the Church*, 5:63.
[29]Genesis 10:25; Doc. & Cov. 133:19-24.
[30]Joseph Fielding Smith, *The Way to Perfection*, p. 309.
[31]Moses 7:61.

PURPOSE OF THE MILLENNIUM

For what purpose is the millennium? Although the Lord has not answered this question specifically in the scriptures, it is evident that the salvation of man is the paramount purpose. There are two means by which opportunities for the salvation of man are continued: First, the salvation of mortals who live during the millennium; and second, the salvation of the dead.

President Brigham Young has pointed out that the millennium is the time when the Saints will build temples and officiate for the dead to a greater extent than ever before.

> Who will possess the earth and all its fulness? Will it not be those whom the Lord has reserved to this honor? And they will come upon Mount Zion as saviors to labor through the millennium to save others. (*Discourses of Brigham Young,* p. 625.)

> And through the millennium, the thousand years that the people will love and serve God, we will build temples and officiate therein for those who have slept for hundreds and thousands of years—those who would have received the truth if they had had the opportunity; and we will bring them up, and form the chain entire, back to Adam. (*Ibid.,* p. 619.)

In the two millennial capitals—the City of Zion, also called the New Jerusalem, and the rebuilt city of Jerusalem—it is ordained that work for the dead be performed in the temples of the Lord.[32] Numerous temples "will appear all over this land—North and

---

[32]Doc. & Cov. 124:36.

South America—and also in Europe and elsewhere," said President Wilford Woodruff.[33]

In brief summation we may say that in the purposes of God for the salvation of His children, provision has been made for the redemption of all. The final dispensation of the gospel, including the millennium, has been reserved for the great work of salvation for the dead. The thousand-year period of peace and righteousness will make it possible for this important service to be accomplished as the tempo of missionary work in the spirit world is increased.

[33]G. Homer Durham, *Discourses of Wilford Woodruff*, p. 163.

Chapter Six

The Spirit World

The standard works of the Church of Jesus Christ of Latter-day Saints give considerable information about the intermediate state between death and the resurrection of the body, but the emphasis upon man's third stage of existence, the spirit world, is secondary to some of the other stages of his existence. Especially is this true of the discussion given on this subject in the Doctrine and Covenants. The references there are generally expressed as a part of some other thought and not as a discussion on the spirit world itself. Generally the association is made with the subject of the resurrection of the body. The reasons for this may be as follows: the spirit world for the hosts of mankind is only temporary. On the other hand, the resurrection of the body is the final and permanent stage of man's eternal existence. The whole gospel plan is designed to bring about the resurrection of man where a fulness of joy is possible.[1]

One of the best statements to be found on how a Latter-day Saint feels about the reality of spirit-consciousness at death was expressed by President Wilford Woodruff in his last will and testament:

> If the laws and customs of the spirit world will permit, I should wish to attend my funeral myself, but

[1]Moses 1:30; Doc. & Cov. 94:33, 34.

I shall be governed by the counsel I receive in the spirit world. (M. F. Cowley, *Wilford Woodruff*, p. 622.)

For us who live in mortality, death of the body and life in the spirit world await us unless we shall be alive when the Savior comes and we are found worthy to be caught up to meet him. Death is one of the realities of which we are all so very well aware. As Latter-day Saints, we may, by the testimony of the Spirit, have an assurance of the reality of the life immediately following the death of the body.

The Spirit of Man

When a Latter-day Saint speaks of the spirit of man, what does he think of? The Lord has revealed that "the spirit of man (is) in the likeness of his person."[2] Yet the spirit is not flesh and bones as the resurrected being,[3] but it is matter that "is more fine or pure, and can only be discerned by purer eyes."[4] The spirit of man was begotten in the heavens before the earth was formed.[5] In that sphere of existence it was in form as man is today, with the ability to walk, talk, think, and act very much as we do today. With birth into mortality the spirit is clothed with grosser matter and gives life to the body. At death of the mortal body the spirit, which is eternal or everlasting, continues its conscious existence as an entity or being with the same form it had in the pre-existent life.

---

[2]Doc. & Cov. 77:2.
[3]*Ibid*, 130:22; Luke 24:39.

[4]Doc. & Cov. 131:7.
[5]*Ibid.*, 76:24.

REALITY OF EVIL SPIRITS

There are evil spirits who are just as real as the spirits of all men who are tabernacled in the flesh. These are the followers of Satan who rebelled with him in the pre-mortal world and are today "seeking to destroy the souls of men."[6] The Prophet Joseph Smith received a revelation in which a key was given whereby we might know how to distinguish between evil and good spirits.[7] This key involves the simple procedure of shaking hands with the visitor from the other side of the veil because of the apparent obsession to deceive on the part of evil spirits. Though of material substance, the hand of the spirit cannot be felt by the mortal. This same revelation also prescribes the manner of detecting the righteous deceased who serve as God's messengers.[7a]

What has come to be a classic example of the reality of the evil forces and their opposition to the work of the Lord in this dispensation is the experience of Elders Isaac Russell, Willard Richards, Orson Hyde, and Heber C. Kimball upon opening the British Mission in 1837. In the words of Elder Kimball:

> I then arose and sat up on the bed, when a vision was opened to our minds, and we could distinctly see the evil spirits, who foamed and gnashed their teeth at us. We gazed upon them about an hour and a half (by Willard's watch). We were not looking towards the window, but towards the wall. Space appeared before us, and we saw devils coming in legions, with their leaders, who came within a few feet of us. They

---

[6]*Ibid.*, 10:27.   [7]*Ibid.*, Sec. 129.   [7a]*Ibid.*, vs. 5-6.

came towards us like armies rushing to battle. They appeared to be men of full stature, possessing every form and feature of men in the flesh, who were angry and desperate; and I shall never forget the vindictive malignity depicted on their countenances as they looked me in the eye; and any attempt to paint the scene which then presented itself, or portray their malice and enmity, would be vain. I perspired exceedingly, my clothes becoming as wet as if I had been taken out of the river. I felt excessive pain, and was in the greatest distress for some time. I cannot even look back on the scene without feelings of horror; yet, by it I learned the power of the adversary, his enmity against the servants of God, and got some understanding of the invisible world. We distinctly heard those spirits talk and express their wrath and hellish design against us. However, the Lord delivered us from them and blessed us exceedingly that day. (Orson F. Whitney, *Life of Heber C. Kimball,* 2nd edition, pp. 130-131.)

Many other witnesses have testified to the reality of the spirit as a conscious being, whether unembodied or disembodied.

Distinction of Terms

It is well to keep in mind that in the scriptures terms are used which sometimes may confuse the reader unless he keeps before him certain distinctions concerning the spirit world and its inhabitants. Those who were faithful in the prexistence and are therefore entitled to an earth life—but yet unborn in mortality—live in the presence of our Eternal Father. We do not include these spirits as inhabitants of the spirit world reserved for those who have lived in mortality and passed on into that stage of existence. There is also the class known as unembodied spirits, already mentioned as the devil and his angels, whose influence is felt by the unforgivable disembodied in the spirit world, but who shall eventually partake of hell with the sons of perdition forever.[8] The devil and his angels are in the spirit state forever, while all other spirit beings will be resurrected. Therefore, the spirit world, or the intermediate state between death and the resurrection will have given up all of its dead when the purposes of God for this earth are accomplished.

THE SPIRIT WORLD—WHERE?

Where is the spirit world about which this chapter is written?

At the funeral of Patriarch James Adams, the Prophet Joseph Smith said that since this good man was now one of the spirits of the just men made perfect, he, "if revealed now, must be revealed in fire," and that:

> The spirits of the just are exalted to a greater and more glorious work: hence they are blessed in their departure to the world of spirits. Enveloped in flaming fire, *they are not far from us,* and know and understand our thoughts, feelings, and emotions, and are often pained therewith. (*History of the Church,* 6:52. Italics author's.)

Brigham Young, Parley P. Pratt and others who

[8]Doc. & Cov. 29:38; *History of the Church,* 1:366.

knew the Prophet have also stated that the spirit world is on or near the earth.

SPIRIT WORLD NOT HEAVEN

All who pass through the change of death go immediately into the spirit world. This was true of Jesus and the penitent thief who expired on the cross also.[9] Latter-day Saints know that the spirit world is not heaven, but the latter term has reference as to the future, to a condition and place following the resurrection. Because of misunderstanding in the world concerning this truth and because of misapplication of the words of Jesus to the penitent thief on the cross, the Prophet Joseph Smith clarified New Testament terms used to describe the spirit world, especially "paradise." Concerning Jesus' words, "Today shalt thou be with me in paradise,"[10] he said that paradise means "the world of spirits" where "the righteous and the wicked all go to the same world of spirits until the resurrection."[11]

SEPARATION OF RIGHTEOUS AND WICKED?

Is it correct to assume that because all the dead go into the same world of spirits, there is not a separation of the just and the unjust?

President Joseph F. Smith taught that in the world of spirits there is a separation of the righteous and the wicked.

[9] I Peter 3:18-20; Alma 40:11.   [11] *History of the Church*, 5:424-425.
[10] Luke 23:43.

The spirits of all men, as soon as they depart from this mortal body, whether they are good or evil, we are told in the Book of Mormon, are taken home to that God who gave them life, where there is a separation, a partial judgment, and the spirits of those who are righteous are received into a state of happiness which is called paradise, a state of rest, a state of peace, where they expand in wisdom, where they have respite from all their troubles, and where care and sorrow do not annoy. The wicked, on the contrary, have no part nor portion in the Spirit of the Lord, and they are cast into outer darkness, being led captive, because of their own iniquity, by the evil one. And in this space between death and the resurrection of the body, the two classes of souls remain in happiness or in misery, until the time which is appointed of God that the dead shall come forth and be reunited both spirit and body, and be brought to stand before God, and be judged according to their works. (*Gospel Doctrine*, 6th ed., p. 448.)

If one studies carefully the Book of Mormon reference upon which the above quotation is based, he will perceive the same truth enunciated by President Smith.[12] The partial judgment received by all men at death is not the final judgment which comes after the resurrection, but its purpose is to bring about the separation of the obedient and the disobedient.[13] An example of judgment and separation is found in the parable of Lazarus and the rich man related by the Savior.[14] In this parable, "Abraham's bosom" is used to denote the place of the righteous dead. The gulf between Lazarus and the rich man which would not

---

[12]Alma 40:11-14.   [14]Luke 16:19-31.
[13]*Gospel Doctrine*, 6th ed., p. 449.

permit passage from the prison or hell and the paradise of the spirit world was bridged by the preaching of the missionaries sent by Jesus, who initiated this work of salvation in the interim between his death and resurrection. The gospel was not preached to the dead before this.[15]

PRISON AND PARADISE

In discussing the beneficent results of the resurrection of the body, the Book of Mormon prophet Jacob indicates that there are localities in the spirit world which are designated "prison" and "paradise."

> And the death of which I have spoken, which is the spiritual death, shall deliver up its dead; which spiritual death is hell; wherefore, death and hell must deliver up their dead, and hell must deliver up its captive spirits, and the grave must deliver up its captive bodies, and the bodies and the spirits of men will be restored one to the other; and it is by the power of the resurrection of the Holy One of Israel.

> O how great the plan of our God! For on the other hand the paradise of God must deliver up the spirits of the righteous, and the grave deliver up the body of the righteous; and the spirit and the body is restored to itself again, and all men become incorruptible, and immortal, and they are living souls . . . (II Nephi 9:12-13.)

President Brigham Young is credited with teaching that both the righteous and the disobedient go to

---

[15]I Peter 3:18-20; 4:6; Joseph Fielding Smith, *The Way to Perfection,* p. 315-317.

prison at death. Upon this point the revisers of the revised edition of the *Doctrine and Covenants Commentary,* who are members of the Council of the Twelve, offer the comment: that "if the word 'prison' is used as a synonym for *hades,* the statement is perfectly correct, for *hades* is understood to be the domain of all the dead. But the righteous and the unrighteous are, of course, not in the same locality in that domain. President Young also explains that the wicked, after death, are unhappy, while the righteous dead have passed beyond the reach of the adversary and are resting in peace until the morning of the resurrection, and this makes it clear that he did not mean to say that all the departed spirits are in the same place or the same condition." (P. 463.)

Heber C. Kimball, counselor in the First Presidency to President Brigham Young, taught the same doctrine:

> Can those persons who pursue a course of carelessness, neglect of duty and disobedience, when they depart from this life, expect that their spirits will associate with the spirits of the righteous in the spirit world? I do no expect it, and when you depart from this state of existence, you will find it out for yourselves. (*Journal of Discourses,* 2:150.)

CHAPTER SEVEN

THE SPIRIT WORLD—Continued

As a Latter-day Saint, what do you expect to see in the spirit world? Is your conception of that world very much different from this state of existence? What conditions, physical and social, exist there?

In the last chapter, consideration was given to the reality of the spirit state, the types of spirits, the location of the spirit world, and the fact that there is a separation of righteous and the wicked. Because much of what we know about that stage of existence is found in the writings of the modern prophets, and their ideas are in the main found in the scriptures, reliance will be put upon this source of information in this chapter.

A VISIT INTO THE SPIRIT WORLD

At the funeral of Jedediah M. Grant, counselor to President Brigham Young, Brother Heber C. Kimball related what Brother Grant had told him about his visit into the spirit world two nights in succession. In this account one will find confirmation of several of the points sustained by the scriptures as they were pointed out in the last chapter. There will also be found a number of additional thoughts pertaining to some of the questions raised at the beginning of this chapter. President Heber C. Kimball said:

I went to see Brother Grant one day last week, and he reached out his hand and shook hands with me. He said to me, "Brother Heber, I have been into the spirit world two nights in succession, and of all the dreads that ever came across me, the worst was to have to again return to my body, though I had to do it. But "O," says he, "the order and government that were there! When in the spirit world, I saw and beheld them organized in their several grades, and there appeared to be no obstruction to my vision; I could see every man and woman in their grade and order. I looked to see whether there was any disorder there, but there was none, neither could I see any death nor any darkness, disorder or confusion." He said that the people he there saw were organized in family capacities; and when he looked at them he saw grade after grade, and all were organized and in perfect harmony. He would mention one item after another and say, "Why, it is just as Brother Brigham says it is; it is just as he has told us many a time."

That is a testimony as to the truth of what Brother Brigham teaches us, and I know it is true from what little light I have.

He saw the righteous gathered together in the spirit world, and there were no wicked spirits among them. He saw his wife; she was the first person that came to him. He saw many that he knew, but did not have conversation with any except his wife, Caroline. She came to him, and he said that she looked beautiful and had their little child, that died on the plains, in her arms, and said, "Mr. Grant, here is little Margaret; you know that the wolves ate her up, but it did not hurt her; here she is all right."

"To my astonishment," Brother Grant said, "when I looked at families there was a deficiency in some, there was a lack, for I saw families that would not be permitted to come and dwell together, because they had not honored their calling here."

He asked his wife, Caroline, where Joseph and Hyrum and Father Smith and others were; she replied they had gone away ahead, to perform and transact business for us. The same as when Brother Brigham and his brethren left Winter Quarters and came here to search out a home; they came to find a location for their brethren.

He also spoke of the buildings he saw there, remarking that the Lord gave Solomon wisdom and poured gold and silver into his hands that he might display his skill and ability, and said that the temple erected by Solomon was much inferior to the most ordinary buildings he saw in the spirit world.

"In regard to gardens," says Brother Grant, "I have seen good gardens on this earth, but I never saw any to compare with those that were there; I saw flowers growing upon one stalk." We have many kinds of flowers on the earth, and I suppose those very articles came from heaven, or they would not be here.

After mentioning the things he had seen, he spoke of how much he disliked to return and resume his body, after having seen the beauty and glory of the spirit world, where the righteous spirits are gathered together. (*Journal of Discourses*, 4:135-136.)

Can Latter-day Saints believe that this is a genuine experience? As in all such experiences there are certain questions which, if answered in the affirmative, verify that accuracy and the reality of the account. These are: (a) Is it in accord with the teachings of the standard works? (b) Does it agree with what the modern prophets have taught? (c) Is it given by persons of responsibility and honesty ?(d) Does the spirit bear witness of it in edification and not darkness?[1]

In this experience it is related that Brother Grant saw in vision his deceased wife and child. This may appear to be inconsistent with the known fact that the spirit of man is an adult when it comes into mortality, and although the mortal body may die in infancy, the spirit is still in size as an adult. President Joseph F. Smith has given us the solution to this problem of the childlike size of the spirit mentioned in the above account.

> The spirits of our children are immortal before they come to us, and their spirits, after bodily death, are like they were before they came. They are as they would have appeared if they had lived in the flesh, to grow to maturity, or to develop their physical bodies to the full stature of their spirits. If you see one of your children that has passed away it may appear to you in the form in which you would recognize it, the form of childhood; but if it came to you as a messenger bearing some important truth, it would perhaps come as the spirit of Bishop Edward Hunter's son (who died when a little child) came to him, in the stature of full-grown manhood, and revealed himself to his father, and said: "I am your son."
>
> Bishop Hunter did not understand it. He went to my father and said: "Hyrum, what does that mean? I

---

[1]Doc. & Cov. 50:17-24; II Nephi 33:1.

buried my son when he was only a little boy, but he has come to me as a full-grown man—a noble, glorious young man—and declared himself my son. What does it mean?

Father (Hyrum Smith), the patriarch told him that the Spirit of Jesus Christ was full-grown before he was born into the world; and so our children were full-grown and possessed their full stature in the spirit, before they entered mortality, the same stature that they will possess after they have passed away from mortality, and as they will also appear after the resurrection, when they shall have completed their mission. (*Gospel Doctrine*, 6th Ed., p. 455.)

WHAT THE SPIRIT WORLD IS LIKE

As to the physical environment, the spirit world is very much like the earth upon which we dwell. The Lord has revealed that vegetation and animal life were created spiritually first, for "all things were before created, but spiritually were they created and made according to my word."[2] The physical creation followed the first spiritual creation. Brother Grant saw flowers beyond his ability to describe, and he also saw buildings which were superior to the buildings he had seen on the earth.

In preaching at the funeral of Elder Thomas Williams (July 19, 1874), President Brigham Young said that in the spirit world we labor and enjoy there many of the same attributes we have here.

When we contemplate the condition of man here upon the earth and understand that we are brought

[2]Moses 3:5-7; Doc. & Cov. 77:2.

forth for the express purpose of preparing ourselves
through our faithfulness to merit eternal life, we ask
ourselves where we are going, what will be our condition, what will be the nature of our pursuits in a state
of being in which we shall possess more vigor and a
higher degree of intelligence than we possess here?
Shall we have labor? Shall we have enjoyment in our
labor? Shall we have any object of pursuit, or shall we
sit and sing ourselves away to everlasting bliss? These
are questions that arise in the minds of people, and they
many times feel anxious to know something about the
hereafter. . . . I would like to say to you, my friends
and brethren, if we could see things as they are, and
as we shall see and understand them, this dark sha-
dow and valley is so trifling that we shall turn around
and look upon it and think, when we have crossed it,
why this is the greatest advantage of my whole existence, for I have passed from a state of sorrow, grief,
mourning, woe, misery, pain, anguish and disappoint-
ment into a state of existence where I can enjoy life
to the fullest extent as far as that can be done without
a body. My spirit is set free, I thirst no more, I want
to sleep no more, I hunger no more, I tire no more, I
run, I walk, I labor, I go, I come, I do this, do that,
whatever is required of me, nothing like pain or weari-
ness, I am full of life, full of vigor, and I enjoy the
presence of my Heavenly Father, by the power of His
Spirit. (*Journal of Discourses* 17:14.)

There are doubtless some things which we do
here that may not be possible in that sphere. Even the
deceased members of the Church of Jesus Christ "have
looked upon the long absence of your (their) spirits
from your (their) bodies to be a bondage."[3] Why is

_____
[3]Doc. & Cov. 45:17.

this? Because there are things which they might not do without the body in the attainment of the exaltation.

DEATH DOES NOT CHANGE ONE'S CHARACTER

Does the transition by death from mortality into the spirit world change one's thinking about the plan of salvation?

It is very evident from the scriptures and the writings of the latter-day prophets that this transition does not change one's attitude and that eventually each person will have to make the necessary changes by the same process which he does here. Amulek, the Book of Mormon prophet, testified to this fact:

> For behold, this life is the time for men to prepare to meet God; yea, behold the day of this life is the day for men to perform their labors.
>
> And now, as I said unto you before, as ye have had so many witnesses, therefore, I beseech of you that ye do not procrastinate the day of your repentance until the end; for after this day of life, which is given us to prepare for eternity, behold, if we do not improve our time while in this life, then cometh the night of darkness wherein there can be no labor performed.
>
> Ye cannot say, when ye are brought to that awful crisis, that I will repent, that I will return to my God. Nay, ye cannot say this; for that same spirit which doth possess your bodies at the time that ye go out of this life, that same spirit will have power to possess your body in that eternal world. (Alma 34:32-34.)

The same spirit of indifference, selfishness, doubt, unteachableness, shiftlessness, and so forth, will possess our spirit bodies in the spirit world, if we have these attitudes when we go out of this life. On the other hand, the virtues which bring joy and happiness will continue with those who have possessed them here. With this doctrine, President Brigham Young was in full accord:

> Suppose, then, that a man is evil in his heart—wholly given up to wickedness, and in that condition dies, his spirit will enter the spirit world intent upon evil. On the other hand, if we are striving with all the powers and faculties God has given us to improve upon our talents, to prepare ourselves to dwell in eternal life, and the grave receives our bodies while we are thus engaged, with what disposition will our spirits enter their next state? They will be still striving to do the things of God, only in a much greater degree—learning, increasing, growing in grace and in the knowledge of the truth. (*Discourses of Brigham Young*, p. 580-581.)

PURPOSE OF SPIRIT WORLD

We may say, then, that the spirit world, as to the salvation of mankind, is the place where all of the spirits of men continue to prepare themselves for their reward according to their works. May it not then be thought of as a place of education, of training in the principles of truth which bring happiness and joy? But in this educative process more time is required for some than for others. Consequently, there shall be some who will not be prepared for the resurrection of the body until at least the thousand years of the millennium have passed away, because they did not prepare themselves while in mortality. It is also evident that these persons are still subject to the evil influence of Satan. On the other hand, the righteous are not in this condition insofar as they have gained the victory over Lucifer here.

> The wicked spirits that leave here and go into the spirit world, are they wicked there? Yes. No matter where they have lived on the face of the earth, all men and women who have died without the keys and powers of the priesthood, though they might have been honest and sincere and have done everything they could, are under the influence of the devil, more or less. Are they as much so as others? No. Take those who were wicked designedly, who knowingly lived without the gospel when it was within their reach, they are given up to the devil; they become tools to the devil and spirits of the devil. Go to the time when the gospel came to the earth in the time of Joseph, take the wicked that have opposed this people and persecuted them to the death, and they are sent to hell. Where are they? They are in the spirit world, and are just as busy as they possibly can be to do everything they can against the prophet and the apostles, against Jesus and his kingdom. They are just as wicked and malicious in their actions against the cause of truth as they were while on the earth. (Brigham Young in *Journal of Discourses,* 3:369-370.)

Thus we see that there are degrees to which a person may be subject to the influence of Satan's hosts. It is also apparent that the eternal principle of free agency is operative in the spirit world.

The freedom to believe and the carrying of traditions and either false or true ideas with one into that life suggests that there can be meetings and gatherings of other religious organizations as there are here today. Eventually, however, all shall come to receive the principles which will give to them an inheritance in one of the kingdoms provided for the resurrected soul. This will, of course, require time and considerable effort. This idea suggests the principal work of the righteous in the spirit world.

WORK IN THE SPIRIT WORLD

The preaching of the gospel in that sphere lies at the basis of the Latter-day Saints' concept of salvation for the dead. The spirit world is the place where those who have not had the opportunity to hear and receive the gospel will be accorded this privilege in keeping with what God has promised since the world began.[4]

The Lord gave a revelation to President Joseph F. Smith, known as the "Vision of the Redemption of the Dead," in which he saw the paradise of the spirit world at the time the Savior organized a missionary corps to preach the gospel to the dead. In this informative revelation, President Smith said:

> I beheld that the faithful elders of this dispensation, when they depart from mortal life, continue their labors in the preaching of the gospel of repentance and

---

[4]Doc. & Cov. 124:33, 40, 41; Isaiah 42:7, 24:17-22; John 5:25, 28.

redemption, through the sacrifice of the Only Begotten Son of God, among those who are in darkness and under the bondage of sin in the great world of the spirits of the dead. (*Gospel Doctrine*, p. 476.)

On another occasion, President Smith said that the good, faithful sisters of this dispensation will also participate in the missionary cause.[5]

Another significant thought was given by President Smith in the "Vision of the Redemption of the Dead" when he recorded that "the dead who repent will be redeemed, through obedience to the ordinances of the house of God, and after they have paid the penalty of their transgressions, and are washed clean, shall receive a reward according to their works, for they are heirs of salvation."[6] In the educative process of redeeming mankind there is the element of punishment because of willful disobedience to known laws of God.[7] The Prophet Joseph Smith defined this punishment:

There is no pain so awful as that of suspense. This is the punishment of the wicked; their doubt, anxiety and suspense cause weeping, wailing and gnashing of teeth. (*History of the Church*, 5:340.)

The great misery of departed spirits in the world of spirits, where they go after death, is to know that they come short of the glory that others enjoy and that they might have enjoyed themselves, and they are their own accusers. (*Ibid.*, 5:425.)

---

[5]*Gospel Doctrine*, p. 461.
[6]*Ibid.*, p. 476.
[7]Doc. & Cov. 19:15-19; Alma 40:13, 14.

Since there is a separation of righteous and wicked in the spirit world, do the repentant dead enjoy the blessings of paradise? President Joseph F. Smith has answered this question in this manner:

> In relation to the deliverance of spirits from their prison house, of course, we believe that can only be done after the gospel has been preached to them in the spirit, and they have accepted the same, and the work necessary to their redemption by the living be done for them. . . . It stands to reason that, while the gospel may be preached unto all, the good and the bad, or rather to those who would repent and to those who would not repeat in the spirit world, the same as it is here, redemption will only come to those who repent and obey. (*Gospel Doctrine*, p. 438.)

Brother Jedediah M. Grant visited paradise or the abode of the righteous spirits, those who had accepted the gospel of Jesus Christ.[8] He saw only loveliness and beauty, happiness and joy, where the Saints of God mingled together in the accomplishment of the Lord's purposes. It would appear consistent with what we know of the great work for the dead that in the spirit world there will be a continuation of the task of gathering genealogical data. No greater opportunity would be available than in that life to preach the gospel to one's progenitors and do genealogical research. Is it not also reasonable that those who will engage in the labor of salvation there will be those who have been interested in the salvation of the souls of men here? This is in accord with what has already

---

[8]Doc. & Cov. 84:49-53.

been presented herein—the same desires, attitudes, etc., which we possess here will bring the blessings of opportunity of further labors with their resultant joy and happiness.

DO THE DEAD RETURN?

"God's house is a house of order, and the spirit world is a room in that house."[9] In the "paradise of God,"[10] Brother Grant saw order and government, people organized in their several grades and families were organized and in perfect harmony.

The principle of order operates in connection with the return of the departed to loved ones on the earth. In the annals of the Church of Jesus Christ of Latter-day Saints it is not uncommon that experiences of this kind are found, attesting to the reality of spirit-consciousness, the perpetuity of life beyond the grave. In a funeral sermon over the remains of Elizabeth H. Cannon (January 29, 1882), President Joseph F. Smith, in speaking to the fact that Jesus had a mission after death, said:

> In like manner our fathers and mothers, brothers, sisters and friends who have passed away from this earth, having been faithful, and worthy to enjoy these rights and privileges, may have a mission given them to visit their relatives and friends upon the earth again, bringing from the divine Presence messages of love,

---

[9]Orson F. Whitney, *Saturday Night Thoughts*, p. 307; Doc. & Cov. 132:8, 18.
[10]Moroni 10:34.

of warning, of reproof and instruction, to those whom they had learned to love in the flesh. And so it is with Sister Cannon. She can return and visit her friends, provided it be in accordance with the wisdom of the Almighty. There are laws to which they who are in the paradise of God must be subject, as well as laws to which we are subject. (*Gospel Doctrine*, p. 436.)

Of such an experience, Parley P. Pratt recorded the appearance of his deceased wife to him as he lay in a Missouri dungeon with but one absorbing thought. "Shall I ever, at any time, however distant it may be, or whatever I may suffer first; shall I ever be free again in this life?" The answer came in this manner:

After some days of prayer and fasting, and seeking the Lord on the subject, I retired to my bed in my lonely chamber at an early hour, and while the other prisoners and the guard were chatting and beguiling the lonesome hours in the upper apartment of the prison, I lay in silence, seeking and expecting an answer to my prayer, when suddenly I seemed carried away in the spirit, and no longer sensible to outward objects with which I was surrounded. A heaven of peace and calmness pervaded my bosom; a personage from the world of spirits stood before me with a smile of compassion in every look, and pity mingled with the tenderest love and sympathy in every expression of the countenance. A soft hand seemed placed within my own, and a glowing cheek was laid in tenderness and warmth upon mine. A well-known voice saluted me, which I readily recognized as that of the wife of my youth, who had for one or two years been sweetly sleeping where the wicked cease from troubling and the weary are at rest. I was made to realize that she was sent to commune with me, and answer my question.

Knowing this, I said to her in a most eager and inquiring tone: Shall I ever be at liberty again in this life and enjoy the society of my family and the Saints, and preach the gospel as I have done? She answered definitely and unhesitatingly: "YES!" I then recollected that I had agreed to be satisfied with the knowledge of that one fact, but now I wanted more.

Said I: Can you tell how, or by what means, or where I shall escape? She replied: "THAT THING IS NOT MADE KNOWN TO ME YET." I instantly felt that I had gone beyond my agreement and my faith in asking this last question, and that I must be content-ed at present with the answer to the first.

Her gentle spirit then saluted me and withdrew. I came to myself. The doleful noise of the guards, and the wrangling and angry words of the old apostate again grated on my ears, but heaven and hope were in my soul.

Next morning I related the whole circumstance of my vision to my two fellow prisoners, who rejoiced exceedingly. This may seem to some like an idle dream, or a romance of the imagination; but to me it was, and always will be, a reality, both as it regards what I then experienced and the fulfillment afterwards. (*Autobiography of Parley P. Pratt,* p. 261, 262.)

Attitude Toward Death

The doctrine of the Church of Jesus Christ of Latter-day Saints gives hope, comfort, and assurance of meeting again with loved ones in the spirit world, where further progress on the way to perfection is available to the faithful. The death of the body, therefore, should hold no permanent sorrow for the

Latter-day Saint. This was well expressed by President Brigham Young at the funeral of his sister, Fanny Young:

> I do not mourn for Sister Fanny: I rejoice. She has lived upwards of three score years and ten, and exhibited the retention of sound sense to her last days with us here. She said to her sister, Nancy, a short time ago, "If you hear of my being dead before you come to see me again, let the first thing you say be 'Hallelujah!'" That remark, to me, evidences the retention of sound judgment. It also appears to me that very many of the Latter-day Saints are as far from good, wholesome ideas and principles, touching their heavenly privileges, as the east is from the west. They covet the riches of the world, craving to serve themselves, to satisfy the sordid disposition within them. Had they the sense of an angel, and were they in possession of mountains of gold, heaped up higher and deeper, broader and longer than these mountains on the east and west of us, they would say, "That vast amount of gold is as nothing when compared with the privilege of even living in this day and age of the world, when the gospel is preached." (*Journal of Discourses*, 7:172.)

CHAPTER EIGHT

"IF A MAN DIE, SHALL HE LIVE AGAIN?"
(Job 14:14)

In the two chapters just considered we should have come more forcibly to recognize that we were dealing with a real world, not one of fancy or imagination. The reality of that existence of which we shall all partake, is attested by the revelations of God as given to His prophets, ancient and modern, and the real waking experiences of men of honesty and responsibility. As you reflect upon that material can you not "feel" the truth of the message given of the realness of the spirit world?

It is the belief of the author that everyone who reads with a sincere desire to know may also receive the same "feeling" about the subject we are to explore in this and the next chapter. The evidence for the resurrection of the body as the Lord has given it to the Latter-day Saints is far beyond the limits of what is known in the world on this important subject. For this, all members of the Church should be profoundly grateful. In the true knowledge of the future life and especially of its reality there is a genuine sense of security which can be a real power for good in one's life.

The lack of faith in revealed knowledge of the future life is apparent in the world. The spirit of materialism, together with the influence of apostate Christian teachings, has taken from the majority of the people the means by which they could more fully understand and have security in the knowledge of the future life.

Belief in Immortality

Attention has already been directed to some surveys of religious belief in the United States and their meaning in Chapter Two. Some of these surveys have indicated that many professed Christians do not have faith in the immortality of the individual at death. In a summary of these surveys published in *This Week Magazine,* March 30, 1952, the following answer to the question "Do most people believe in immortality?" was given: "Yes. Nationwide surveys, again covering all creeds, show that more than three people out of four believe in life hereafter. Eleven per cent are uncertain, and 13 per cent believe that when you die you're dead, and that's all there is to it. It is interesting to note that though 94 per cent of the people believe in God, only 76 per cent believe in immortality." Again, we might raise the question as to what extent a person's belief in God (and consequently in the immortality of the individual) influences a person's daily behavior. (See Chapter Two.) In the article just quoted an answer to this question may be found in a survey of men and women in 18 different colleges and universities over the country. It was found that in this group, 61 per cent of the students felt very definitely that their daily conduct was strongly influenced by their belief in God, but the other 39 per cent felt that it made little or no difference.* Most of these 39 per cent professed a strong belief in God, however.

What the World Needs

Whatever reservation one may have concerning surveys of public opinion in giving a completely accurate picture, it is evident that a great many professing believers in Deity do not believe in the immortality of the individual, nor does religious belief necessarily influence one's daily behavior. It should, therefore, be apparent that what the world needs is a new witness for God and revelation from Him to give mankind a basis for belief in immortality.† This has been the message of Joseph Smith and his successors to the world for over a century now, but approximately only two million people have received it.

What evidence is there that the resurrection is a reality?

Inasmuch as Latter-day Saints have superior grounds for belief in the immortality of man, it might

---

*Another survey of college students indicated on virtually all questions on religious belief, seniors expressed greater skepticism than freshmen, with the exception of belief in immortality.

†In some extensive surveys of 10 countries, including the United States, as to belief in God, it was found that Brazil ranked first, with 96 per cent believing in God; the United States was fourth, while the lowest was France, with 66 percent.

be profitable to divide the answer to this question into two parts: the evidence which is common to every Christian, and that which is known only to Latter-day Saints.

Common Evidence of the Resurrection

As to the first, we may suggest the testimony of witnesses to the resurrection of Jesus Christ, for upon Jesus' resurrection rests the eventual resurrection of all mankind. The Savior arose from the dead and appeared to many. Over a period of forty days, he communed with his chosen apostles and others, being seen and heard. Elder James E. Talmage listed eleven recorded appearances of Christ between his resurrection and ascension. Numbered among these testators were Mary Magdalene, Peter, and James to whom the Lord came on separate occasions. There were times when the Lord appeared to two persons and also to five hundred.[1] Subsequent to the Lord's ascension into heaven, the most notable witness is Paul, who testified that, "last of all he was seen of me."[2] Both Paul and Peter did not declare themselves as witnesses alone, but almost invariably they declared that the evidence rested upon the testimony of all the apostles.[3]

Many have suggested that the zeal with which the apostles of the Lord undertook their divine calling as special witnesses of the Savior following his resurrec-

---

[1]*Jesus the Christ,* p. 699.
[2]I Cor. 15:8.
[3]*Ibid.,* 15:3-9; Acts 2:32; 3:15; 10:41.

tion is an evidence which cannot be discounted as a verification that something very vital came into their lives. The fact that these men went to martyr's graves for the knowledge that Jesus lives as a tangible, resurrected being, is strong evidence for this argument.

In addition to the foregoing evidence for the resurrection, Latter-day Saints have superior basis for knowing that the immortality of the body through the atonement of Jesus is an assured fact. Many in the world disbelieve the actual resurrection of Christ, and others[4] because the record of those events is of such antiquity and the literal resurrection is something which requires considerable faith to accept. On the other hand, Latter-day Saints need not be concerned with either one of these problems.

L.D.S. EVIDENCE OF JESUS' EXISTENCE

One of the purposes of the Doctrine and Covenants is to give evidence of the reality of the future life. This is done in two ways. First, by the testimonies of men who have seen the resurrected Christ. Three persons testify to a sight-knowledge of the Savior. Joseph Smith and Oliver Cowdery beheld the glorified Lord in the Kirtland Temple, on April 3, 1836. This is their account of that event:

> The veil was taken from our minds, and the eyes of our understanding were opened.
> We saw the Lord standing upon the breastwork of

---

[4]Matthew 27:52, 53.

the pulpit, before us; and under his feet was a paved work of pure gold, in color like amber.

His eyes were as a flame of fire; the hair of his head was white like the pure snow; his countenance shone above the brightness of the sun, and his voice was as the sound of the rushing of great waters, even the voice of Jehovah, saying:

I am the first and the last; I am he who liveth, I am he who was slain; I am your advocate with the Father. (Doc. & Cov. 110:1-4.)

When Joseph Smith and Sidney Rigdon saw the celestial world, it was their privilege to see Jesus and to hear the voice of God the Father declare Him to be His Only Begotten Son:

And while we meditated upon these things, the Lord touched the eyes of our understandings and they were opened, and the glory of the Lord shone round about.

And we beheld the glory of the Son, on the right hand of the Father, and received of his fulness;

And saw the holy angels, and them who were sanctified before his throne, worshipping God, and the Lamb, who worship him forever and ever.

And now, after the many testimonies which have been given of him, this is the testimony, last of all, which we give of him: That he lives!

For we saw him, even on the right hand of God; and we heard the voice bearing record that he is the Only Begotten of the Father—

That by him, and through him, and of him, the worlds are and were created, and the inhabitants thereof are begotten sons and daughters unto God. (*Ibid.*, 76:19-24.)

APPEARANCE OF RESURRECTED BEINGS

The second way in which the Doctrine and Covenants evidences the truth of the future life is by testifying to the reality of the resurrection. This is done in two ways: by giving considerable knowledge about the resurrection (to be given in the next chapter) and by giving specific information concerning the appearance of resurrected beings in our day. Some of these messengers from the heavens conversed with Joseph Smith and Oliver Cowdery in the conferring of keys of authority necessary for the work of the Dispensation of the Fulness of Times.

Moroni, the ancient American prophet, "being dead, and raised again therefrom, appeared unto me," said Joseph Smith.[5] Upon numerous occasions, Moroni conversed with him about his part in the restitution of all things, and delivered the gold plates into his hands.[6]

John the Baptist, forerunner of Jesus in the Meridian of Time, conferred the Aaronic Priesthood upon Joseph Smith and Oliver Cowdery.[7]

Peter and James, as resurrected beings, with John, a translated being,[8] appeared to Joseph Smith and

---

[5]*Elders Journal*, Far West, Mo., July, 1838.
[6]Doc. & Cov. 2:1-3, and introductory note; 27:5, P. of G. P., Joseph Smith 2:30-60.
[7]Doc. & Cov., Sec. 13, and introductory note; 27:7, 8; 133:55.
[8]*Ibid.*, Sec. 7.

Oliver Cowdery and conferred the Melchizedek Priesthood.[9]

Moses, the great law-giver of ancient Israel, restored the keys of the gathering of Israel and the restoration of the ten tribes from the land of the north to Joseph and Oliver.[10]

Elias, a prophet who apparently lived in the days of Abraham, delivered the keys of the gospel of Abraham.[11]

Elijah, the prophet who was carried into heaven without tasting of death but who later underwent a change to the resurrected state at the time of Jesus' resurrection,[12] committed the keys of the sealing power of the priesthood.[13]

These were resurrected personages (except for the Apostle John, who had a translated body), bringing great blessings for mankind and at the same time attesting to the literalness of the resurrection and the reality of the immortality of the body.

VISITATION OF ANGELS

Joseph Smith mentions other holy messengers who may have been resurrected or as just men made perfect in the spirit state ministering in accordance with their rights and privileges.

[9]*Ibid.*, 27:12, 13; 128:20.
[10]*Ibid.*, 110:11; 133:55.
[11]*Ibid.*, 110:12; 27:6.
[12]*Ibid.*, 133:55.
[13]*Ibid.*, 110:13-16; 27:9; 128:17, 18.

And again, the voice of God in the chamber of old Father Whitmer, in Fayette, Seneca county, and at sundry times, and in divers places through all the travels and tribulations of this Church of Jesus Christ of Latter-day Saints! And the voice of Michael, the archangel; the voice of Gabriel, and of Raphael, and of divers angels, from Michael or Adam down to the present time, all declaring their dispensation, their rights, their keys, their honors, their majesty and glory, and the power of the priesthood; giving line upon line, precept upon precept; here a little, and there a little; giving us consolation by holding forth that which is to come, confirming our hope! (*Ibid.*, 128:21.)

In bearing testimony to the divine mission of Joseph Smith as a prophet, President John Taylor spoke of his greatness in the pre-mortal world and that God had selected him as the prophet of the last dispensation of the gospel. Then President Taylor gave this significant statement:

I know of what I speak, for I was very well acquainted with him and was with him a great deal during his life, and was with him when he died. The principles which he had, placed him in communication with the Lord, and not only with the Lord, but with the ancient apostles and prophets; such men, for instance, as Abraham, Isaac, Jacob, Noah, Adam, Seth, Enoch, and Jesus and the Father, and the apostles that lived on this continent as well as those who lived on the Asiatic continent. He seemed to be as familiar with these people as we are with one another. Why? Because he had to introduce a Dispensation of the Fulness of Times, and it was known as such by the ancient servants of God. (*Journal of Discourses*, 21:94.)

The Book of Mormon as a Witness

In addition to the purpose of the Doctrine and Covenants as a testifier of the reality of the resurrection, new revelation in the form of an ancient book comes to man as a new witness that God is mindful of his children in other parts of the world than where the Bible was produced. The principal purpose of the Book of Mormon is to verify the divinity of Jesus Christ as the Son of God and Savior of Mankind. This is done in several ways, among which is the historical fact that Jesus Christ was actually raised from the dead and appeared to the faithful people upon this continent in the first Christian century. The dramatic appearance of the Savior to the Nephites as recorded in the eleventh chapter of III Nephi is a marvelous testimony of the truth of the Book of Mormon. As the multitude looked upward "they saw a Man descending out of heaven; and he was clothed in a white robe," whereupon he introduced himself as the Lord Jesus Christ.[14] The resurrected Lord spoke unto them saying: ". . . thrust your hands into my side, and also that ye may feel the prints of the nails in my hands and in my feet, that ye may know that I am the God of Israel, and the God of the whole earth, and have been slain for the sins of the world." One by one the multitude "did see with their eyes and did feel with their hands, and did know of a surety and did bear

---

[14]III Nephi 11:8.

record, that it was he, of whom it was written by the prophets, that should come."[15]

Moroni, last mortal custodian of the Book of Mormon plates, was an eyewitness of the resurrected Jesus about 400 years later. In bidding farewell to the future readers of the Book of Mormon, he referred to the time when all should meet before the judgment seat of Christ, "And then shall ye know that I have seen Jesus, and that he hath talked with me face to face, and that he told me in plain humility, even as a man telleth another in mine own language, concerning these things."[16]

In the area of personal manifestations evidencing the reality of the resurrection and of the future life, aside from specific teachings about immortality, Latter-day Saints have a further witness in Joseph Smith's First Vision. Joseph Smith saw God! Jesus Christ is a resurrected personage, separate and distinct from the father. That He who once was dead now lives is a message of the First Vision![17]

Do you feel as a Latter-day Saint that we have superior reasons for faith in the existence of God? Do you have faith in the Savior as a resurrected Personage, and feel that the resurrection is not a figment of the imagination? Is this "feeling," belief, or faith sufficiently strong to make of you a genuine follower of the Master in daily conduct, in contrast to the many who profess belief but do not genuinely follow?

---

[15]*Ibid.*, 11:14-15.
[16]Ether 12:39-41.
[17]P. of G. P., *Writings of Joseph Smith*, 2:11-25.

Final Evidence

The final evidence which a Latter-day Saint has of the reality of the future life is the positive knowledge which comes from the Holy Ghost. This is superior knowledge given to the faithful members of The Church of Jesus Christ of Latter-day Saints. The Prophet Joseph Smith encouraged us to:

> Search the scriptures—search the revelations which we publish and ask your Heavenly Father, in the name of His Son Jesus Christ, to manifest the truth unto you, and if you do it with an eye single to His glory, nothing doubting, He will answer you by the power of His Holy Spirit. You will then know for yourselves and not for another. You will not then be dependent on man for the knowledge of God; nor will there be any room for speculation. (*Teachings of the Prophet Joseph Smith*, pp. 11-12.)

The means by which this is possible are available to Latter-day Saints. Each member has had hands laid on his head for the reception of the Holy Ghost. The Prophet said that "no man can receive the Holy Ghost without receiving revelations. The Holy Ghost is a revelator."[18] President Heber J. Grant, seventh president of the Church, said about the right of revelation to the members of the Church:

> The Lord gives to many of us the still, small voice of revelation. It comes as vividly and strongly as though it were with a great sound. It comes to each man, according to his needs and faithfulness, for guidance in matters that pertain to his own life. For the Church as a whole it

---

[18]*Teachings of the Prophet Joseph Smith*, p. 328.

comes to those who have been ordained to speak for the Church as a whole. This certain knowledge which we have that the guiding influence of the Lord may be felt in all the ways of life, according to our needs and faithfulness, is among the greatest blessings God grants unto men. With this blessing comes the responsibility to render obedience to the "still small voice." (*Improvement Era*, 41:712.)

This kind of experience constitutes a "hidden treasure."[19]

---

[19]Doc. & Cov. 89:19.

CHAPTER NINE

THE RESURRECTION OF THE BODY

In setting forth the evidence of the resurrection from the Doctrine and Covenants it was indicated in the last chapter that in addition to the testimonies of men of honesty who saw the resurrected Christ and messengers of God who had been raised from the dead, there is considerable information in the modern revelations about the subject of the resurrection. It is the purpose of this chapter to use this material of the ancient prophets and also the writings of the modern prophets in learning what superior knowledge the Latter-day Saints possess on this important subject.

TESTIMONY OF THE PROPHETS BEFORE CHRIST

The prophets in all dispensations have looked forward to the time when death would be removed permanently and the blessings of eternal life would then be available to the faithful sons and daughters of God. Probably one of the best Old Testament references on this is the 19th verse of the 26th chapter of Isaiah:

Thy dead men shall live, together with my dead body shall they arise. Awake and sing, ye that dwell in dust: for thy dew (*death or sorrow*) is as the dew of herbs, (*it shall quickly pass away as dew passes away by the rays of the morning sun*), and the earth shall cast out the dead. (Words in italics author's.)

The testimony of Job,[1] of Ezekiel,[2] and of Daniel[3] also express this idea from the ancient prophets. Book of Mormon prophets before the birth of Jesus testified by the spirit that there would be a resurrection. Among these are: Abinadi,[4] Amulek,[5] Jacob,[6] Alma,[7] and Samuel.[8]

JESUS THE FIRST TO BE RESURRECTED

In many of these testimonies reference is made to the fact that the resurrection would come to Jesus Christ first and that by the power of God through the atonement of His Son others would participate in this blessing.

New Testament writers attested to the Savior's resurrection as the first, in expressions as "the first fruits of them that slept,"[9] "first begotten of the dead,"[10] "first born from the dead,"[11] and "the first that should rise from the dead."[12] The emergence of Jesus from the tomb as a symbol of hope is widely acknowledged in Christendom and forms the basis of the Easter observance.[13]

Biblical accounts of raising the dead before the time of Jesus' resurrection, such as the instances when Elijah[14] and Elisha[15] performed this miracle, the rais-

[1]Job 19:25-27.
[2]Ezekiel 37:1-14.
[3]Daniel 12:2.
[4]Mosiah 16:7-10.
[5]Alma 11:41-44.
[6]II Nephi 9:6-8, 11-13.
[7]Alma 40:21-23.
[8]Helaman 14:15, 16.

[9]I Cor. 15:20.
[10]Rev. 1:5.
[11]Colossians 1:15.
[12]Acts 26:23.
[13]John 20:1-18.
[14]I Kings 17:17-24.
[15]II Kings 4:31-37.

ing of Lazarus,[16] the young man of Nain,[17] and the daughter of Jarius,[18] have given some people concern. As Elder James E. Talmage has pointed out, these miracles are restorations to life and not resurrections. The difference is that in these cases the individuals would again die, while the resurrected being is immortal.[19] Jesus was the first of this earth to be resurrected.

RESURRECTION OF FLESH AND BONES

The account of His coming from the sepulchre and subsequent events plainly testify to the literalness of Jesus' resurrection. He was raised with the same body which was put into the tomb, but it had become glorified and immortal. As the disciples were gathered together, the risen Lord asked them to "behold my hands and my feet, that it is I myself: handle me, and see; for a spirit hath not flesh and bones, as ye see me have."[20] At a later date, in the presence of the eleven apostles, the Master asked Thomas to feel His hands and thrust his hand into His side. Thomas exclaimed: "My Lord and my God."[21] His appearance to others as revealed in the scriptures witness that he was a personal Being with a body of flesh and bones.

Jesus Christ was the pattern of the resurrection.[22] The resurrection of which we shall partake will be the raising of the body as flesh and bones — tangible,

[16]John 11:1-46.
[17]Luke 7:11-17.
[18]Mark 5:22-24, 35-43.
[19]*Jesus the Christ,* pp. 316, 495-496.

[20]Luke 24:39.
[21]John 20:27, 28.
[22]I John 3:2; Doc. & Cov. 130:22

material substance.[23] This body will not consist of blood,[24] but, as Joseph Smith said: "All will be raised by the power of God, having spirit in their bodies and not blood."[25] The spirit referred to can only mean a substitute for blood and not the spirit, which is a separate entity in itself. President Brigham Young declared:

> The blood will not be resurrected with the body, being designed only to sustain the life of the present organization. When that is dissolved, and we again obtain our bodies by the power of the resurrection, that which we now call the life of the body, and which is formed from the food we eat and the water we drink will be supplanted by another element. (*Discourses of Brigham Young*, p. 573.)

This explains why the scriptures refer to the resurrected body as "a spiritual body"[26] or as Amulek put it, "the whole becoming spiritual and immortal."[27] In this condition man will not be subject to decay or dissolution, but will remain free from disease and the ills of earth life or mortality. The prophets have spoken of this condition as "incorruptible."[28]

THEY CAN DIE NO MORE

The thought is sometimes expressed that it is possible for a person because of a sin unto death while

---

[23]Philippians 3:20, 21; Alma 11:43-45; Doc. & Cov. 129:1, 2.
[24]I Cor. 15:50.
[25]*History of the Church*, 4:555.
[26]Doc. & Cov. 88:27; I Cor. 15:35, 44.
[27]Alma 11:45.
[28]I Cor. 15:52; II Nephi 9:13.

in mortality to be resurrected and then for the spirit and the body to be separated again as in the first death. This teaching is not in accord with what the prophets have revealed in the scriptures. When once resurrected, the person remains forever united—spirit and body—"inseparably connected,"[29] "they can die no more; their spirits uniting with their bodies, never to be divided; thus the whole becoming spiritual and immortal, that they can no more see corruption."[30] The "second death"[31] is banishment from the presence of God, and not the dissolution of the resurrected body.[32]

PERFECT BODIES

As resurrected beings we shall have perfect bodies. The disfigurements of the flesh will be removed. A question is sometimes raised as to whether or not there will be a difference in the resurrection between the person who dies in young adulthood and the one who leaves mortality at an advanced age. The scriptures do not speak expressly to this question, but only of the perfected body. The Prophet Joseph Smith said that "they differ in stature, in size, the same glorious spirit gives them the likeness of glory and bloom; the old man with his silvery hairs will glory in bloom and beauty."[33] Elder B. H. Roberts taught that:

> We shall live, believe me, not in decrepit, wornout or deformed bodies, but in bodies restored to the full

[29]Doc. & Cov. 93: 33.
[30]Alma 11:45; Doc. & Cov. 63:49.
[31]Rev. 20:5, 6; Doc. & Cov. 76:37.

[32]Ibid., 29:41; Alma 12:16-18.
[33]History of the Church, 6:366.

stature of the spirits they are to clothe. We shall inhabit them erect and strong and young and unwrinkled;
with every power increasing and developing through
all the ages in which we shall live. The Christ is the type
of the resurrection; and he was raised at about 33 years
of age in the perfection of his manly beauty and powers, and so ultimately shall it be with men. If not immediately raised to it, he shall attain unto it." ("The
'Falling Away' or the World's Loss of the Christian Religion and Church," radio series, KSL, 1929)

The Book of Mormon prophets Amulek and Alma
testified that the spirit and body would be reunited
again in its perfect form.[34]

The Prophet Joseph Smith is reported as saying:
"As concerning the resurrection, I will merely say that
all men will come from the grave, as they lie down,
whether old or young; there will not be 'added unto
their stature one cubit,' neither taken from it; all will
be raised by the power of God, having spirit in their
bodies, and not blood."[35]

President Joseph F. Smith gave this testimony
regarding the resurrection:

The death that came by the fall of our first parents
is eradicated by the resurrection of the Son of God, and
you and I cannot help it. You will come forth from your
graves, these same mortal bodies as they are now,
bearing the marks just as much as Christ's body bore
the marks that were upon him. They will come forth
from their graves, but they will be immediately immor-

---

[34]Alma 11:43, 44; 40:23.
[35]*History of the Church,* 4:555.

talized, restored to their perfect frame, limb, and joint. And the poor, unfortunate creature who has lost a leg or an arm or a finger will have it restored to its proper frame, every joint to its place, and every part to its part, and it will be made perfect, for that is the law of restoration that God has instituted by which His own purpose cannot fail, by which His own designs concerning His children must be consummated. Now this is the restoration I believe in. What is more desirable than that we should meet with our fathers and our mothers, with our brethren and our sisters, with our wives and our children, with our beloved associates and kindred in the spirit world, knowing each other, identifying each other by the marks we knew in the flesh and by the associations that familiarize each to the other in mortal life? What do you want better than that? What is there for any religion superior to that? I know nothing." (*Liahona the Elder's Journal*, Vol. 6, No. 8, p. 178)

Some Latter-day Saints believe that the opportunity for a faithful Latter-day Saint mother to rear her deceased child will come in the spirit world. This is not correct, however, because the spirit of the infant is an adult in form (see Chapter Seven). The Prophet Joseph Smith taught that the fulfilment of this promise will come in the resurrection, as expressed in these words of President Joseph F. Smith:

Joseph Smith declared that the mother who laid down her little child being deprived of the privilege, the joy, and the satisfaction of bringing it up to manhood or womanhood in this world, would, after the resurrection, have all the joy, satisfaction, and pleasure, and even more than it would have been possible to have had in mortality, in seeing her child grow to the full

measure of the stature of its spirit. (*Gospel Doctrine,*
p. 453; Cf. *History of the Church,* 4:555-557.)

RESURRECTION OF FUNDAMENTAL PARTS

Many professing Christians believe that the resurrection does not mean a literal raising of the body from
the grave, but the new life as a spirit apart from the
body constitutes the Biblical resurrection. As already
indicated in this chapter, this is a belief not in accord
with the Bible. At the basis of this erroneous thought,
in part at least, is the difficulty which some people
have in believing that the decomposed body can be
restored. On the other hand, there are those who may
accept a literal resurrection, but who cannot subscribe
to the doctrine that the fundamental elements which
compose the mortal body are to be raised from the
resting place. Admittedly, there are a number of
things which the Lord has not yet made known to
man about how certain things can be done. We have
his promise, as Latter-day Saints, however, that we
shall come to understand these matters.[36]

The Prophet Joseph Smith was emphatic in main-
taining that in the resurrection we do not lose the
fundamental parts of the body which were ours in
mortality:

> There is no fundamental principle belonging to a
> human system that ever goes into another in this world
> or in the world to come; I care not what the theories of
> men are. We have the testimony that God will raise us

[36]Doc. & Cov. 101:32-34.

up, and he has the power to do it. If anyone supposes
that any part of our bodies, that is, the fundamental
parts thereof, ever goes into another body, he is mis-
taken. (*History of the Church,* 5:339.)

This doctrine was taught by Brigham Young, Joseph F. Smith, and other successors of the Prophet.

In suggesting an answer to the question of what
are the fundamental parts of the body, Elder Harold
B. Lee of the First Presidency quoted a physician to
the effect that our bodies are composed of elements
some of which are used and discarded and new sub-
stances come to take their place. But there are parts
which do not change. "People may live on their own
tissues until they become almost 'skin and bone,' yet
they live and can, when fed again, regain their former
form and weight. During the fast, the fundamental
parts of the body are not lost, but only the tissues that
are taken into the body temporarily."[37]

SOME THINGS NOT UNDERSTOOD

It should be an obvious fact to all that there are
a great many questions about our environment and
life itself which are unknown notwithstanding the
great advances which science has made through the
will of our Father in heaven. If it were necessary for
us to understand many of the elemental things about
us before we enjoyed them, we would find ourselves
in a precarious position. This idea was very well ex-

[37]*Youth and the Church,* p. 191, 192.

pressed by William Jennings Bryan in his renowned speech "The Prince of Peace":

> And our food, must we understand it before we eat it? If we refused to eat anything until we could understand the mystery of its growth, we would die of starvation. But mystery does not bother us in the dining room; it is only in the church that it is a stumbling block.
>
> I was eating a piece of watermelon some months ago and was struck with its beauty. I took some of the seeds and dried them and weighed them, and found that it would require some five thousand seeds to weigh a pound; and then I applied mathematics to that forty-pound melon. One of these seeds, put into the ground, when warmed by the sun and moistened by the rain, takes off its coat and goes to work. It gathers from somewhere two hundred thousand times its own weight, and forcing this raw material through a tiny stem, constructs a watermelon. It ornaments the outside with a covering of green; inside the green it puts a layer of white, and within the white a core of red, and all through the red it scatters seeds, each one capable of continuing the work of reproduction. Who drew the plan by which that little seed works? Where does it get its tremendous strength? Where does it find its coloring matter? How does it collect its flavoring extract? How does it develop a watermelon? Until you can explain a watermelon, do not be too sure that you can set limits to the power of the Almighty and say just what He would do or how He would do it. (*The Prince of Peace,* pp. 24-26.)

In the same area of the presently "unknown" and yet substantiated by present-day example are these properties of the resurrected body: it is not bound to earth by gravitation, nor do material barriers hinder its movements, and it may be visible or invisible to us mortals. The risen Lord rendered Himself invisible to two disciples with whom he dined.[38] Was it necessary to roll away the great stone which covered the opening of the Lord's tomb in order for Him to have an exit on the resurrection day? Elder James E. Talmage has pointed out these properties in this manner:

> A resurrected body, though of tangible substance, and possessing all the organs of the mortal tabernacle, is not bound to earth by gravitation, nor can it be hindered in its movements by material barriers. To us who conceive of motion only in the directions incident to the three dimension of space, the passing of a solid, such as a living body of flesh and bones, through stone walls, is necessarily incomprehensible. But that resurrected beings move in accordance with laws making such passage possible and to them natural, is evidenced not only by the instance of the risen Christ, but by the movement of other resurrected personages. Thus, in September, 1823, Moroni, the Nephite prophet who had died about 400 A.D., appeared to Joseph Smith in his chamber three times during one night, coming and going without hindrance incident to walls or roof. (See P. of G. P., Joseph Smith, 2:43; also *The Articles of Faith*, i:15-17.) That Moroni was a resurrected man is shown by his corporeity manifested in his handling of the metallic plates on which was inscribed the record known to us as the Book of Mormon. So also resurrected beings possess the power of rendering themselves visible or invisible to the physical vision of mortals. (*Jesus the Christ*, p. 698.)

---

[38]Luke 24:13-35.

CHAPTER TEN

THE FUTURE KINGDOMS

The Lord has revealed that every person who has lived upon the earth will receive a resurrection. This means both the "just and unjust,"[1] "death and hell delivered up the dead which were in them,"[2] "all shall be made alive."[3] By reason of the transgression of Adam death entered the world, and through the atonement of Jesus Christ all mankind will be redeemed from this temporal death. There is no exception.[4]

MANY RESURRECTIONS

The general scriptural pronouncement is that there is a time for the righteous and a time for the unrighteous to be raised from the grave.[5] The resurrection of all mankind is in general put into two classifications—the first or of the "just" and the second or of the "unjust." A modern revelation, however, teaches us that these general classifications should be separated into two parts each.[6] Each one of these resurrections, four in number, is known in this revelation by the sounding of an angel's trump.

---

[1]Acts 24:15.
[2]Rev. 20:13.
[3]I Cor. 15:21-22.
[4]II Nephi 9:6, 7, 12, 13; Alma 12:16-18.
[5]Rev. 20:5, 12, 13; Doc. & Cov. 29:22-26.
[6]Doc. & Cov. 88:97-102.

The first trump at the Savior's coming:

> And they who have slept in their graves shall come forth, for their graves shall be opened; and they also shall be caught up to meet him in the midst of the pillar of heaven—

> They are Christ's, the first fruits, they who shall descend with him first, and they who are on earth and in their graves, who are first caught up to meet him; and all this by the voice of the soundings of the trump of the angel of God. (Doc. & Cov., 88:97-98.)

The second trump is sounded after the resurrection of the Saints. The length of time between these two events is not revealed. Jesus' coming marks the beginning of the millennium, therefore, the resurrection of terrestrial beings occurs after the millennium begins:

> And after this another angel shall sound, which is the second trump; and then cometh the redemption of those who are Christ's at his coming; who have received their part in that prison which is prepared for them, that they might receive the gospel, and be judged according to men in the flesh. (Doc. & Cov. 88:99.)

Thus ends the first general resurrection, except as that resurrection will continue into the millennium until all the worthy or honorable dead have received this blessing. At the end of the thousand years of peace and righteousness, the second general resurrection will begin with telestial beings rising from their graves:

And again, another trump shall sound, which is the third trump; and then come the spirits of men who are to be judged, and are found under condemnation;

And these are the rest of the dead; and they live not again until the thousand years are ended, neither again, until the end of the earth. (*Ibid.*, 88:100-101.)

Without the time interval being indicated, the last part of the last or second resurrection, that of the sons of perdition, is described as follows:

And another trump shall sound, which is the fourth trump, saying: There are found among those who are to remain until that great and last day, even the end, who shall remain filthy still. (*Ibid.*, 88:102.)

VISIONS OF THE RESURRECTION

There are still some items concerning the resurrection of the body which will be considered in later chapters. Further evidence for and information about these general resurrections have been made known by vision to two prophets of this dispensation.

The Prophet Joseph Smith's account is as follows:

Would you think it strange if I relate what I have seen in vision in relation to this interesting theme? Those who have died in Jesus Christ may expect to enter into all that fruition of joy when they come forth, which they possessed or anticipated here.

So plain was the vision, that I actually saw men, before they had ascended from the tomb, as though they were getting up slowly. They took each other by the hand and said to each other, "My father, my son, my mother, my daughter, my brother, my sister." And when the voice calls for the dead to arise, suppose I am laid by the side of my father, what would be the first joy of my heart? To meet my father, my mother, my brother, my sister; and when they are by my side, I embrace them and they me.

All your losses will be made up to you in the resurrection provided you continue faithful. By the vision of the Almighty I have seen it.

More painful to me are the thoughts of annihilation than death. If I have no expectation of seeing my father, mother, brothers, sisters and friends again, my heart would burst in a moment, and I should go down to my grave.

The expectation of seeing my friends in the morning of the resurrection cheers my soul and makes me bear up against the evils of life. It is like their taking a long journey, and on their return we meet them with increased joy.

God has revealed His Son from the heavens and the doctrine of the resurrection also; and we have a knowledge that those we bury here God will bring up again, clothed upon and quickened by the Spirit of the great God; and what mattereth it whether we lay them down, or we lie down with them when we can keep them no longer? Let these truths sink down in our hearts, that we may even here begin to enjoy that which shall be in full hereafter. (*Teachings of the Prophet Joseph Smith,* pp. 295-296.)

As President of the Church, Wilford Woodruff related a vision of the resurrection given to him while laboring as a missionary in the state of Tennessee during the lifetime of Joseph Smith. Note that in this vision, President Woodruff describes the second general resurrection, the first having already occurred.

After laboring in that part (Memphis, Tennessee) for a length of time, I received a letter from Joseph Smith and Oliver Cowdery, in which they requested me to stay in that country and take charge of the churches that we had built up there. The Prophet promised me many things, and said I would lose no blessings by tarrying in that country and doing as he wished me, and letting the other brethren go and get their endowments. I was then at the house of Brother Abraham O. Smoot's mother. I received this about sundown. I went into a little room where there was a sofa, to pray alone. I felt full of joy and rejoicing at the promises God had made to me through the Prophet. While I was upon my knees praying, my room was filled with light. I looked and a messenger stood by my side. I arose, and this personage told me he had come to instruct me. He presented before me a panorama. He told me he wanted me to see with my eyes and understand with my mind what was coming to pass in the earth before the coming of the Son of Man. He commenced with what the revelations say about the sun being turned to darkness, the moon to blood, and the stars falling from heaven. Those things were all presented to me one after another, as they will be, I suppose, when they are manifest before the coming of the Son of Man. Then he showed me the resurrection of the dead—what is termed the first and second resurrection. In the first resurrection I saw no graves nor anyone raised from the grave. I saw legions of celestial beings, men and women who had received the gospel all clothed in white robes. In the form they were presented to me, they had already been raised from the grave. After this he showed me what is termed the second resurrection. Vast fields of graves were before me, and the Spirit of God rested upon the earth like a shower of gentle rain, and when that fell upon the graves, they were opened, and an immense host of human beings came forth. They were just as diversified in their dress as we are here, or as they were laid down. This personage taught me with regard to these things . . .

I refer to this as one of the visitations that was given me in my boyhood, so to speak, in the gospel. I was a priest at the time. Of course, there was a motive in this personage visiting me and teaching me these principles. He knew a great deal better than I did what lay before me in life. It was doubtless sent me for the purpose of strengthening me and giving me encouragement in my labors. (*The Deseret Weekly*, Vol. 53, No. 21, November 7, 1896, p. 642.)

ETERNAL MAN AND HIS OPPORTUNITIES

These visions of the resurrection emphasize the fact expressed so often in the scriptures that the human personality persists beyond the grave. The further fact that there are differences between individuals is clearly marked in the revealed word of God. These differences existed in the premortal life; they are here in mortality; and they will continue into the hereafter.[6a] Because of this, one finds varying degrees of obedience to gospel principles and laws. The various stages through which man travels—pre-existence, earth life, spirit world—are intended to prepare man for the resurrected life, where he receives his reward in accordance with eternal laws. Because of a reign

---

[6a]Joseph Fielding Smith, *Way to Perfection*, p. 50.

of law in the universe, man enjoys security. If he lives the law, blessings follow.[7]   On the other hand, if man persists in wrongdoing, he suffers the penalty of the broken law:

> And again, verily I say unto you, that which is governed by law is also preserved by law and perfected and sanctified by the same.
>
> That which breaketh a law, and abideth not by law, but seeketh to become a law unto itself, and willeth to abide in sin, and altogether abideth in sin, cannot be sanctified by law, neither by mercy, justice, nor judgment. Therefore, they must remain filthy still. (Doc. & Cov. 88:34-35.)

Through suffering, man is cleansed and by his repentance the benefits of the atonement for individual salvation, varying as it does between persons, are made available to him.[8]   It has already been pointed out (Chapter Seven) that the spirit world is the place where men continue to work out their salvation in accordance with their opportunities in mortality. Whatever man does not do here in this educative process, he must do in that sphere of action. Consequently, the prophets, ancient and modern, have counseled that now is the day of salvation, and "do not procrastinate the day of your repentance until the end," for the change of death does not alter one's character.[9]   Heber C. Kimball expressed this thought as follows:

---

[7]Doc. & Cov. 130:20, 21; 82:10.
[8]*Ibid.*, 19:15-19.
[9]Alma 34:33-35.

Have I not told you often that the separation of the body and spirit makes no difference in the moral and intellectual condition of the spirit? . . . The spirit has not changed one single particle of itself by leaving the body. (Orson F. Whitney, *Life of Heber C. Kimball*, p. 462.)

Doctrine of Overcoming

This principle has given rise to what might be termed the doctrine of "overcoming." It is given by Brother Kimball in these words:

If you do not cultivate yourselves, and cultivate your spirits in this state of existence, it is just as true as there is a God that liveth you will have to go into another state of existence, and bring your spirits into subjection there. Now you may reflect upon it, you will never obtain your resurrected bodies, until you bring your spirits into subjection. I am not talking to this earthly house of mine, neither am I talking to your bodies, but I am speaking to your spirits. I am not talking as to people who are not in the house. Are your spirits in the house? Are not your bodies your houses, your tabernacles or temples, and places for your spirits? Look at it; reflect upon it. If you keep your spirits trained according to the wisdom and fear of God, you will attain to the salvation of both body and spirit. I ask, then, if it is your spirits that must be brought into subjection? It is, and if you do not do that in those bodies, you will have to go into another estate to do it. You have got to train yourselves according to the law of God, or you will never obtain your resurrected bodies. (*Ibid.*, p. 459.)

President Brigham Young said that everyone must undergo preparation for his final destiny:

No spirit of Saint or sinner of the Prophet or him that kills the Prophet, is prepared for their final state; all pass through the veil from this state and go into the world of spirits; and there they dwell waiting for their final destiny. (*Discourses of Brigham Young*, p. 576.)

All men will be made "vessels unto honor," except the sons of perdition, but on the basis of principles to which they could have subjected themselves while in mortality, given the opportunity. Of the wilful sinner, Brother Kimball expresses this fact:

The spirits of the Saints will be gathered in one, that is, of all who are worthy; and those who are not just, will be left where they will be scourged, tormented and afflicted, until they can bring their spirits into subjection and be like clay in the hands of the potter, that the potter may have power to mould and fashion them into any kind of vessel, as he is directed by the Master Potter. (*Life of Heber C. Kimball*, p. 464.)

SALVATION DEFINED

In the final analysis, this doctrine of "overcoming" is what Joseph Smith defined as salvation:

Salvation is nothing more nor less than to triumph over all our enemies and put them under our feet. And when we have power to put our enemies under our feet in this world, and a knowledge to triumph over all evil spirits in the world to come, then we are saved, as in the case of Jesus, who was to reign until He had put all enemies under His feet, and the last enemy was death. (*Teachings of the Prophet Joseph Smith*, p. 297.)

As to individual salvation, then, we are not saved

in this life, but we, by obedience to the plan of life and salvation, are on the way to perfection or to one of the great kingdoms of the future. The "unsaved" are spoken of as being "in bondage,"[10] while the "saved" have "overcome" and are "free."[11]

By the resurrection, man has reached a point where he has power over the devil and his angels who have not received bodies of flesh and bones.

> The spirits in the eternal world are like the spirits in this world. When those have come into this world and received tabernacles, then died and again have risen and received glorified bodies they will have an ascendancy over the spirits who have received no bodies, or kept not their first estate, like the devil. The punishment of the devil was that he should not have a habitation like men. The devil's retaliation is, he comes into this world, binds up men's bodies, and occupies them himself. When the authorities come along, they eject him from a stolen habitation. (*History of the Church*, 5:403.)

SUMMARY

In recapitulation: Man, a child of God, is an eternal being who enjoys free agency. Our Father in heaven places him in various stages of progression whereby he may "work out his salvation" in accordance with laws which give happiness if lived, but remorse if not lived. The spirit world is the last stage of final preparation. Each person will have to subject himself to laws of righteousness in order to receive

---

[10]II Peter 2:19, 20.
[11]Rev. 2:7, 26; John 8:32.

the resurrection. (Sons of perdition are the exception.) Resurrected men will have power over unembodied evil spirits.

THE GREATNESS OF GOD'S PLAN

The creeds of men, developed over the centuries without revelation from heaven, have pictured God as banishing the sinner forever into a hell where punishment is endured eternally. This doom is believed to be incurred by the vast majority of mankind. The notion that there was only "heaven" and "hell," without an intermediate state of preparation for immortality or resurrection, gave rise to a doctrine of salvation incompatible with the teachings of the gospel of Jesus Christ. The saved were wafted into heaven, while the sinner went to hell, lost forever.

In contradiction to this erroneous and unjust concept of God's justice, the message of the Church of Jesus Christ of Latter-day Saints proclaims the doctrine that our Father in heaven is solicitous for all of His children and has provided the means whereby they may receive, if not all, a measure of His glory. This, however, comes only by their placing themselves in accord with divine laws either in mortality or in the spirit world. In the words of a modern revelation, we learn:

> And this is the gospel, the glad tidings, which the voice out of the heaven bore record unto us—
>
> That he came into the world, even Jesus, to be crucified for the world, and to bear the sins of the

world, and to sanctify the world and to cleanse it from
all unrighteousness;

That through him all might be saved whom the
Father had put into his power and made by him;

Who glorifies the Father, and saves all the works
of his hands, except those sons of perdition who deny
the Son after the Father has revealed him.

Wherefore, he saves all except them. . . . (Doc &
Cov., 76:40-44.)

SONS OF PERDITION

The few, known as sons of perdition, constitute
an infinitesimal number of all of our Father's children. The number has not been revealed, but there
will be "many apostates of the Church of Jesus Christ
of Latter-day Saints who will receive this condemnation."[12] The sin which brings this condemnation of
everlasting punishment where they dwell with Satan
and his angels forever,[13] is called the sin against the
Holy Ghost.[14] Perhaps the most explicit statement
concerning this group was given by the Prophet:

All sins shall be forgiven, except the sin against the
Holy Ghost; for Jesus will save all except the sons of
perdition. What must a man do to commit the unpardonable sin? He must receive the Holy Ghost, have
the heavens opened unto him, and know God, and then
sin against Him. After a man has sinned against the
Holy Ghost, there is no repentance for him. He has
got to say that the sun does not shine while he sees it;

---

[12]*Teachings of the Prophet Joseph Smith,* p. 358.
[13]Doc. & Cov. 76:44.
[14]Matt. 12:31, 32.

> he has got to deny Jesus Christ when the heavens have
> been opened unto him, and to deny the plan of salvation
> with his eyes open to the truth of it; and from that time
> he begins to be an enemy. This is the case with many
> apostates of The Church of Jesus Christ of Latter-day
> Saints. (*Teachings of the Prophet Joseph Smith*, p. 358;
> cf. Doc. & Cov. 76:31-35; 132:27.)

"The unpardonable sin is to shed innocent blood,
or be an accessory thereto." (*DHC* 5:391.)

For these and the unembodied followers of Satan,
the Prophet had this to say concerning their fate:

> Say to the brothers Hulet and to all others, that the
> Lord never authorized them to say that the devil, his
> angels, or the sons of perdition, should ever be restored;
> for their state of destiny was not revealed to man, is not
> revealed, nor ever shall be revealed, save to those who
> are made partakers thereof: consequently those who
> teach this doctrine have not received it of the Spirit of
> the Lord. (*Teachings of the Prophet Joseph Smith*, p.
> 24; Cf. Doc. & Cov. 76:45-48.)

The sons of perdition will be resurrected to "abide
a kingdom which is not a kingdom of glory,"[15] where
they suffer the second death, or "as to things pertaining
unto righteousness" but as resurrected beings "they
cannot die, seeing there is no more corruption."[16]

Although Lucifer and his angels are called sons
of perdition, the spirit who has come to earth life for
a body and then, by death of the body, enters into

---

[15]Doc. & Cov. 88:24, 32.
[16]Alma 12:16-18; Doc. & Cov. 29:41; 76:36-38.

the spirit world, "cannot commit the unpardonable sin." It is a sin, as to mortals, which is possible while in the mortal tabernacle.[17]

WORK FOR THE DEAD

Provision is made that every soul shall have an opportunity to receive the fulness of the gospel, if not in mortality, then in the spirit world. In Chapter Seven, consideration was given briefly to the work of preaching the gospel to the departed dead. Temples of the Lord are constructed in order that our kindred dead might receive the beneficial ordinances of the celestial kingdom. It was pointed out, however, that man's free agency is preserved in every stage of his eternal journey and therefore many will not avail themselves of these saving principles and ordinances.

HELL IS REAL

Notwithstanding what is given herein concerning the broad, liberal ideas of man's salvation when contrasted with the general notion of limited salvation to a few while the vast host of mankind are doomed to hell forever, one must never lose sight of the fact that there is a real hell for the unrepentant. This does not refer to the hell mentioned in the scriptures for the sons of perdition. The wicked of the earth shall be in the prison house of the spirit world—"thrust down to

---

[17]*Teachings of the Prophet Joseph Smith*, p. 357.

hell . . . not to be redeemed from the devil until the last resurrection."[18]

GRADUATIONS TAUGHT IN BIBLE

The magnanimity of the gospel of Jesus Christ as revealed in our generation far transcends the uninspired conception of men. This is well illustrated in what has been presented with reference to the salvation of all men upon which more will be given in the next chapter. That there are graduations in "heaven" was taught by Jesus[19] and by his disciples, one of which was Paul, who received a vision of the kingdoms of glory for resurrected man:

> There are also celestial bodies, and bodies terrestrial; but the glory of the celestial is one, and the glory of the terrestrial is another.
>
> There is one glory of the sun, and another glory of the moon, and another glory of the stars: for one star differeth from another star in glory. (I Cor. 15:40-41.)

The principles of reward and punishment is given in this New Testament scripture: "He which soweth sparingly shall reap also sparingly; and he which soweth bountifully shall reap also bountifully."[20]

---

[18]Doc. & Cov. 76:84-85, 106.
[19]John 14:1, 2; Doc. & Cov. 98:18.
[20]II Cor. 9:6.

CHAPTER ELEVEN

THE FUTURE KINGDOMS—Continued

We have learned that through the restoration of the gospel, Joseph Smith gave to the world a different concept of the hereafter from the one entertained in the creeds of men brought about by a lack of divine revelation. In this chapter we shall consider what the modern revelations teach concerning the three heavens or degrees in which the vast host of mankind will be saved. We have learned of the fourth kingdom, one not of glory, in the last chapter.

NO ADVANCEMENT UPWARD

Prepared in the spirit world for the resurrection, each person will rise from the grave with a body suited to dwell in one of the great kingdoms of the future.

> They who are of a celestial spirit shall receive the same body which was a natural body; even ye shall receive your bodies, and your glory shall be that glory by which your bodies are quickened.
>
> Ye who are quickened by a portion of the celestial glory shall then receive of the same, even a fulness.
>
> And they who are quickened by a portion of the terrestrial glory shall then receive of the same, even a fulness.

And also they who are quickened by a portion of the telestial glory shall then receive of the same, even a fulness.

And they who remain shall also be quickened; nevertheless, they shall return again to their own place, to enjoy that which they are willing to receive, because they were not willing to enjoy that which they might have received. (Doc. & Cov. 88:28-32.)

This fact suggests that when resurrected and assigned to one of these kingdoms, there is no advancement upward from one kingdom to another.[1] This does not apply only to those of the telestial kingdom, but to all of the kingdoms.[2] Divine law specifies that if one does not abide the law of one of the future kingdoms, he cannot abide that glory.[3]

The specific ordinances, if there be such, which will be required for entrance into the terrestrial or telestial kingdoms have not been revealed. The initiatory ordinances of water baptism and the laying on of the hands for the gift of the Holy Ghost, and other ordinances known to us, are for *only* the celestial kingdom.

Telestial Kingdom

Of the lowest of the kingdoms of glory, the *telestial*, the Lord has said that there are innumerable gradations or degrees in it:

[1]Doc. & Cov. 76:112.
[2]*Ibid.*, 93:26-28.
[3]*Ibid.*, 88:20-24.

> And the glory of the telestial is one, even as the glory of the stars is one; for as one star differs from another star in glory, even so differs one from another glory in the telestial world. (*Ibid.*, 76:98; I Cor. 15:41.)

In this kingdom of glory will be assigned those who, in these chapters, have been referred to as the wicked of the earth—liars, sorcerers, adulterers. They are those who rejected the gospel and the testimony of Jesus and the prophets. They were the followers of man-made systems, who persisted in their abominable ways.[4] It is these who will come from their graves in the first part of the second or general resurrection at the end of the millennium. (Chapter Ten.)

Although coming under this condemnation, they have been cleansed in the spirit world and are prepared to enter a glory "which surpasses all understanding."[5] In their kingdom they will receive the administration of angels and of the Holy Spirit.[6]

According to the vision given to Joseph Smith and Sidney Rigdon, the majority of those who lived on the earth will inherit the telestial glory:

> But behold, and lo, we saw the glory and the inhabitants of the telestial world, that they were as innumerable as the stars in the firmament of heaven, or as the sand upon the seashore. (Doc. & Cov. 76:109.)

---

[4]*Ibid.*, 76:99-106, 81-85.
[5]*Ibid.*, 76:89.
[6]*Ibid.*, 76:88, 86.

Terrestrial Kingdom

Above the telestial world is that of the *terrestrial kingdom,* likened to the moon in contrast to the brightness of the stars, which typify the telestial glory. They who receive this kingdom, "excel in all things the glory of the telestial, even in glory, and in power, and in might, and in dominion." But they are below the celestial world as the sun differs from the moon.[7]

Differing from the telestial inhabitants, terrestrial beings are those who "are honorable men of the earth, who were blinded by the craftiness of men." These lived the moral teachings of the gospel, but they did not receive the fulness on the earth nor in the spirit world. In this kingdom there will also be those who "died without the law."[8] Concerning the latter, the Lord has declared that they constitute the heathen nations:

> And then shall the heathen nations be redeemed, and they that knew no law shall have part in the first resurrection; and it shall be tolerable for them. (*Ibid.,* 45:54.)

In addition to those mentioned, there shall be some Latter-day Saints who were honorable in their lives, but who were indifferent to the fulness of the truth. Expressed in the language of the revelation, they were "not valiant in the testimony of Jesus; wherefore they obtain not the crown over the king-

[7]*Ibid.,* 76:91, 92, 96-98, 71.
[8]*Ibid.,* 76:72-75.

dom of our God."⁹ It was their privilege to obtain that crown, but the spirit of apathy toward the work of the Lord gained ascendancy in their lives.

Although the revelations do not speak directly to the question as to whether there will be degrees or gradations in this kingdom, as it does of the telestial and the celestial, it is apparent that because there are differences in the works of righteousness of those in that kingdom that there are such gradations.

Terrestrial beings will minister to the inhabitants of the telestial world.¹⁰

Is the Gospel Narrow?

When Latter-day Saint missionaries explain the position of the Church with reference to other Christian churches, it is not infrequent that they are charged with being narrow and intolerant. This thought is expressed in this way: "Then you believe that since your Church is the only true Church, all the rest of us Christians are wrong, and therefore lost?"

Without setting forth all of the possible replies to this question, it is apparent to the Latter-day Saint who knows of the doctrine of salvation, that the Church of Jesus Christ of Latter-day Saints is neither narrow nor intolerant. All men may worship as they choose without hindrance on our part. The gospel is not narrow in what it teaches concerning the good,

---

⁹*Ibid.,* 76:69.
¹⁰*Ibid.,* 76:86.

honorable Christian who receives the privilege of accepting the fulness of the gospel, if not on the earth then in the spirit world.

There is probably no better answer to this charge of narrowness than what is given to us concerning the honorable to inherit the terrestrial kingdom. This answer is based on the Christian's idea of God and the hereafter. It is maintained that there is only one being in the Godhead, who is known as Jesus Christ the Savior, and the blessings of the hereafter will be the joy of being in His presence forever. The honorable Christian will be in the presence of Jesus Christ; consequently the "Christian's" goal will be realized provided his was an honorable life:

> These are they who receive of his glory, but not of his fulness.
>
> These are they who receive of the presence of the Son, but not of the fulness of the Father.
>
> Wherefore, they are bodies terrestrial, and not bodies celestial, and differ in glory as the moon differs from the sun. (*Ibid.*, 76:76-78.)

The *present* concept of "heaven" of the honorable Christian will be realized! Can it, therefore, be truthfully maintained that the Church of Jesus Christ of Latter-day Saints is narrow and intolerant because it teaches that it is "the only true and living church upon the face of the whole earth?"[11] In the light of

---
[11]*Ibid.*, 1:30.

what has just been given, what do we mean when
we say there is only one true Church?

MEANING OF ONE TRUE CHURCH

Joseph Smith received from God the *fulness* of the
gospel of Jesus Christ. He who lives it has the promise from the Lord that "all that my Father hath shall
be given unto him."[12] All others will receive a lesser
portion of what the Father has, commensurate with
the degree to which they have obeyed principles of
righteousness.

There are gradations of the celestial kingdom to
accommodate different levels of adherence to the
gospel among the members of the Church of Jesus
Christ. This fact is clearly established in these words:

> In the celestial glory there are three heavens or
> degrees;
>
> And in order to obtain the highest, a man must
> enter into this order of the priesthood [meaning the
> new and everlasting covenant of marriage]:
>
> And if he does not, he cannot obtain it.
> He may enter into the other, but that is the end of
> his kingdom; he cannot have an increase. (*Ibid.*, 131:
> 1-4.)

The line is drawn as clearly between the highest
and the other two degrees or levels of the celestial
kingdom as between the telestial, terrestrial, and celestial kingdoms.

---

[12]*Ibid.*, 84:39.

ETERNAL LIFE OR EXALTATION

Latter-day Saints who do not receive all of the ordinances of salvation are not candidates for the highest heaven in the celestial kingdom. The ordinance of celestial marriage or marriage for eternity is the qualifying ordinance, followed by keeping the covenants of that divine contract and the preparatory covenants in the temple endowment. The temple marriage for eternity makes it possible for a man and a woman, as husband and wife to realize the great objective of God's work—eternal life.[13]

What power separates those who gain exaltation and those of a lesser kingdom of glory, or even those in the celestial kingdom? It is the power or ability to have "increase"[14] or spirit children.

> Except a man and his wife enter into an everlasting covenant and be married for eternity, while in this probation, by the power and authority of the Holy Priesthood, they will cease to increase when they die; that is, they will not have any children after the resurrection. (Joseph Smith, *History of the Church*, 5:-391.)

Synonyms for "eternal increase" are "enlarged," "continuation of the seeds forever and ever," "the exaltation and continuation of the lives."[15] The opposite of this condition is expressed as "wide is the way that leadeth to the deaths,"[16] or the inability to

---

[13]Moses 1:39.
[14]Doc. & Cov. 131:4.
[15]*Ibid.*, 132:17-19, 22.
[16]*Ibid.*, 132:25.

have spirit children. This power marks the difference between those who attain godhood and all others, including those in the celestial kingdom who become angels; "therefore, they cannot be enlarged, but remain separately and singly, without exaltation, in their saved condition, to all eternity; and from henceforth are not gods, but are angels of God forever and ever."[17]

BASIS OF SALVATION FOR THE DEAD

The blessings of the celestial kingdom will not be denied anyone who is worthy to receive them. As pointed out in these chapters, God's justice allows that those who did not have the opportunity will receive it. This glorious truth lies at the foundation of our understanding of salvation for the dead. The Prophet Joseph Smith beheld in vision the celestial kingdom, about which he wrote:

> The heavens were opened up on us, and I beheld the celestial kingdom of God, and the glory thereof, whether in the body or out I cannot tell. I saw the transcendent beauty of the gate through which the heirs of that kingdom will enter, which was like unto circling flames of fire; also the blazing throne of God, whereon was seated the Father and the Son. I saw the beautiful streets of that kingdom, which had the appearance of being paved with gold . . . Thus came the voice of the Lord unto me saying—
>
> All who have died without a knowledge of this gospel, who would have received it if they had been

[17]*Ibid.*, 132:17.

permitted to tarry shall be *heirs* of the celestial kingdom
of God; also all that shall die henceforth without a
knowledge of it, who would have received it with all
their hearts, shall be *heirs* of that kingdom, for I, the
Lord, will judge all men according to their works, according to the desire of their hearts. (*Teachings of the
Prophet Joseph Smith*, p. 107. Italics author's.)

It is only through obedience to the gospel of Jesus
Christ that man will receive the celestial kingdom. It
is only by obedience to the fulness of the gospel of
Jesus Christ that man may reach the heights of godhood.[18]

SALVATION OF CHILDREN

In the plan of salvation, it is contemplated that *all*
children, regardless of race, color, or creed, who die
before they reach the age of accountability, eight
years, are saved in the celestial kingdom through the
atonement of Jesus Christ.[19] The voice of the Lord to
Joseph Smith was heard to say in the vision:

And I also beheld that all children who die before
they arrive at the years of accountability, are *saved* in
the celestial kingdom of heaven. (*Teachings of the
Prophet Joseph Smith*, p. 107. Italics author's.)

This is what Jesus meant when He blessed little
children and said that they were of the kingdom of
heaven.[20] A number of latter-day prophets have dis-
coursed upon this subject. Among these was President
Lorenzo Snow, who at the funeral of a little boy, said:

---

[18]Doc. & Cov. 132:28-33; 93:26-28; 130:20, 21.
[19]*Ibid.*, 68:25-28; 29:46, 47; 74:7.
[20]Matt. 18:1-6.

Now, this little boy [four and one-half year old son of Heber J. Grant] has not lived through the years that others have, and that he might have lived, provided, as I think, that it was in the providence of God. Well, he goes back there, having been cut short of living as long as the usual time of people. He will receive as much honor and as much glory and be welcomed there as having accomplished that for which he came into the world, and for which he was willing to come into the world. That is all that could be required, and wherein could there posibbly be any loss? I can see none, and I am just as positive that in time to come or in eternity this little fellow will not be cut short in its powers. It may require a great many years, it may go into the thousands, but you will see that little fellow growing up and becoming enlarged, his capacity increasing as opportunities are furnished him, and he will start a kingdom, and that kingdom will increase. His posterity will increase and become as numerous as the seashore, or as the stars in the firmament, and he will rule over them, and give them instructions, as the Lord now governs and controls us, His offspring, so he will govern and control his offspring. I am sure of these things. (*Millennial Star* 57:387, June 20, 1895.)

Celestial beings shall have part in the resurrection of the just and will dwell in the presence of God and Christ forever and ever.[21] Because children dying before eight years of age (and these constitute a great number) will be found in the celestial kingdom, that kingdom will consist of "an innumerable company,"[22] and yet they will be few compared with the great number of God's children who belong to this earth.[23]

------

[21]Doc. & Cov. 76:62-64.   [22]*Ibid.*, 76:67.   [23]Matt. 7:13, 14.

Chapter Twelve

"It Is Finished"
(Doc. & Cov. 88:106)

In this dispensation the Lord has renewed the promise made known to earlier prophets[1] that righteousness shall triumph over evil and the faithful sons and daughters of God will receive an everlasting inheritance.

> And by hearkening to observe all the words which I, the Lord their God, shall speak unto them, they shall never cease to prevail until the kingdoms of the world are subdued under my feet, and the earth is given unto the saints, to possess it forever and ever. (Doc. & Cov. 103:7.)
>
> . . . it is decreed that the poor and the meek of the earth shall inherit it. (*Ibid.*, 88:17.)

The "end of the earth" will come as the final stage of the Lord's work for the salvation of man.[2] This end, however, is not a destruction of the earth that it will be no more, but because it "filleth the measure of its creation, and transgresseth not the law" it shall be sanctified and "the righteous shall inherit it."[3] No other people will reside on the glorified earth except celestial beings. Those of other kingdoms must abide

---

[1]Daniel 7:27; Matt. 5:5.
[2]Doc. & Cov. 29:22-25; 43:31.
[3]*Ibid.*, 88:25.

other places than the earth, the whereabouts of which the Lord has not revealed.

At that time the earth will be celestialized and in its perfected form will serve as a means whereby its inhabitants will learn of the hidden mysteries of the Lord's kingdom which will be revealed unto them, "even the wonders of eternity shall they know, and things to come will I show them, even the things of many generations."[4] The earth will be as a "sea of glass"[5] to reveal things of a lower kingdom than the celestial.

> This earth, in its sanctified and immortal state, will be made like unto crystal and will be a Urim and Thummim to the inhabitants who dwell thereon, whereby all things pertaining to an inferior kingdom, or all kingdoms of a lower order, will be manifest to those who dwell on it; and this earth will be Christ's. (Doc. & Cov., 130:9.)

But of the celestial kingdom knowledge will come through the medium of a white stone:

> Then the white stone mentioned in Revelation 2:17, will become a Urim and Thummim to each individual who receives one, and whereby things pertaining to a higher order of kingdoms will be made known;

> And a white stone is given to each of those who come into the celestial kingdom, whereon is a new name written, which no man knoweth save he that receiveth it. The new name is the key word. (Doc. & Cov. 130:10-11.)

[4]*Ibid.*, 76:5-10.
[5]*Ibid.*, 77:1.

Before the celestialization of the earth and as the millennium draws to an end, Lucifer, who has been bound during the thousand years of peace and righteousness on the earth, will gather together his forces for the final conflict. Numbered among his armies will be those on the earth who will "deny their God."[6] And Michael (Adam),[7] the seventh angel, even the archangel, shall gather together his armies, even the hosts of heaven."[8] Satan and his armies, the hosts of hell, will come up to battle against Michael and his armies.

> And then cometh the battle of the great God; and the devil and his armies shall be cast away into their own place, that they shall not have power over the saints any more at all.
>
> For Michael shall fight their battles, and shall overcome him who seeketh the throne of him who sitteth upon the throne, even the Lamb. (*Ibid.*, 88:114-115.)

With the final defeat of the devil and his followers, they will be cast into hell which was prepared for them from the beginning.[9]

As the end draws near, the final resurrection will occur, as indicated by various angels' trumps discussed in Chapter Ten. The last to be resurrected are the sons of perdition, upon the sounding of the fourth trump. These shall remain "until that great and last day, even the end, who shall remain filthy still."[10]

[6]Doc. & Cov. 29:22.
[7]*Ibid.*, 27:11.
[8]*Ibid.*, 88:112.

[9]*Ibid.*, 29:38; 76:44.
[10]*Ibid.*, 88:102.

In succession, without the time interval between the events given, the following series of trumps are sounded:[11]

Fifth trump: Moroni, who delivered the gold plates to Joseph Smith, will deliver this message to all people in heaven and on the earth: "Fear God, and give glory to him who sitteth upon the throne, forever and ever; for the hour of his judgment is come."

Sixth trump: The proclamation is given that error and untruth led the nations to destruction.

Seventh trump: The glorious message is given that Jesus the Lamb of God has overcome, and therefore *it is finished, it is finished*. With this announcement the angel shall "be crowned with the glory of his might, and the saints shall be filled with his glory, and receive their inheritance and be made equal with him."

In the introductory chapter, three principal messages of the Doctrine and Covenants were stated. In this concluding chapter it is proposed that consideration be given to a summary of these messages as they have been developed in this book.

Message One — A Warning to the World

We are living in a wonderful age. Significant changes in man's material well-being have been made

---
[11]*Ibid.,* 88:103-107.

by science. A noted theoretical physicist has pointed out some of these changes.

> Advances in the study of man and other living forms have extended our life span by decades. Discoveries in physical science have immeasurably lightened our toil, and enriched our lives. They have given leisure to an ever-widening group of men. They have made a reasonable education not a special privilege, but a common right. They have made the world in its physical dimensions, a small place, and established the means by which people in remote parts of the earth can communicate with each other, can get to know each other, and can learn to work together. They have put at the disposal of everyone the resources of physical power, of ease, and of knowledge that were in the past reserved for the few. ("Encouragement of Science," *Bulletin of the Atomic Scientists*, January 1951, p. 6.)

The exploration of the moon is one of the rewarding scientific achievements of our age.

Latter-day Saints recognize in this progress the fulfilment of what Joel, the Old Testament prophet, said would occur in the latter days—the Lord would pour out His "spirit upon all flesh."[12] This would be one of the signs of the Dispensation of the Fulness of Times, which began with the restoration of visions as a form of revelation.

It is apparent from the complete text that this prophecy would be fulfilled in the latter days, although God would give His spirit in the dispensation following Joel's time. Joel's prophecy of our dispensation is:

---

[12]Joel 2:28.

And it shall come to pass afterward, that I will pour out my spirit upon all flesh; and your sons and your daughters shall prophesy, your old men shall dream dreams, your young men shall see visions:

And also upon the servants and upon the handmaids in those days will I pour out my spirit.

And I will shew wonders in the heavens and in the earth, blood, and fire, and pillars of smoke.

The sun shall be turned into darkness, and the moon into blood, before the great and the terrible day of the Lord come.

And it shall come to pass, that whosoever shall call on the name of the Lord shall be delivered: for in Mount Zion and in Jerusalem shall be deliverance, as the Lord has said, and in the remnant whom the Lord shall call. (*Joel* 2:28-32.)

The Angel Moroni quoted these verses to Joseph Smith the night of his first visit to him and said "that this was not yet fulfilled, but was soon to be."[13] It should be observed that a number of the signs prophesied by the Savior (see Chapter Two) are included in this prophecy. It appears that Moroni wanted to impress upon Joseph Smith's mind that this was the beginning of the last days and that the world would have a "voice of warning" in the form of various signs.[14]

The reference in Joel to deliverance from these judgments was discussed in Chapter Five, with par-

---

[13]P. of G. P., Joseph Smith 2:41.
[14]Doc. & Cov. 88:88-91

ticular regard to the Latter-day Saints. In Chapter
Four consideration was also given to the places of
gathering as well as information about the Jewish
remnant.

The Lord has definitely said that these are the
last days and that terrible judgments await the world
if repentance is not accepted. The influence of the
great apostasy, the deception by Lucifer[15] have
brought a spirit of unbelief with its attendant evils.
(See Chapter One.) A profession of belief in God,
but obedience to his laws is lacking. The great advances made by science, as indicated above, have
made many put their trust in the arm of flesh, man,
to the exclusion of God, as a real influence in their
lives. (Chapter Two.)

The material advancement that man has made
in the decades past has also brought forth a flood
of articles and predictions about the future of our
civilization.

In retrospect the editor of the *Bulletin of the
Atomic Scientists;* writing five years after the first
issue of this magazine appeared, writes as follows:

> The first issue of the *Bulletin of the Atomic Scien-
> tists* appeared on December 15, 1945. It was born of a
> combination of gloom and hope. Standing around the
> first nuclear fire lit under the West Stands of the
> Athletic Field of the University of Chicago in Decem-
> ber, 1942, and two and a half years later, in July, 1945,

---

[15]*Ibid.*, 10:24-27.

watching the flash of the first atomic bomb explosion at Alamogordo, the scientists had a vision of terrible clarity: They saw the cities of the world, including their own, falling into dust and going up in flames. They saw that human history had but to remain true to the pattern it has followed for thousands of years— a sequence of wars interrupted by brief interludes of peace—for our civilization, which we had heretofore believed to be the first stage of an ultimate and universal civilization of mankind (different—we thought—from the local civilizations of the past, that rose and became stagnant and disintegrated), to end in chaos and destruction, the like of which had not been seen on earth. In the summer of 1945, some of us walked the streets of Chicago vividly imagining the sky suddenly lit by a giant fireball, the steel skeletons of skyscrapers bending into grotesque shapes and their masonry raining into the streets below, until a great cloud of dust rose and settled over the crumbling city. (January, 1951, p. 3.)

It was hoped that "the fate of Hiroshima and Nagasaki would cause man to turn a new leaf." The publication of this bulletin was a part of these efforts to persuade him to do so. However, "the patient is steadily getting worse." A world's armament race is still in progress in which more destructive ways of killing man are being sought. "What then have we to show for five years of effort, except the relief of having 'spoken and saved our souls' — and the doubtful satisfaction of having been right in our gloomy predictions?"[16]

Although "the great and terrible day of the Lord"

[16]*Bulletin of the Atomic Scientists,* January, 1951, p. 5.

—for those who are not prepared (Chapters Three and Four)—will come, and the wicked shall not stand, the Latter-day Saint, trusting in the promises of the Lord, looks forward to a future filled with hope (Chapter Five). If this is not realized in mortality, the blessings of happiness and eternal advancement are possible in the hereafter.[17a]

MESSAGE TWO—(A) THE EVENTS OF THE FUTURE

The signs of the times are to prepare those who will heed them for the coming of the Lord Jesus Christ in power and glory. This preparation should be going on now in the lives of the members of The Church of Jesus Christ of Latter-day Saints. This Church is fulfilling its divine mission by having the gospel preached to as many as will listen. The work of redeeming the dead by providing temples for faithful members to officiate in behalf of their deceased relatives continues. Large expenditure of funds is being made to collect genealogical data for this purpose. The third objective of the Church is also being carried forward—the provision through Church service and other opportunities to help the members perfect their lives. The inspired leadership in the Church continues to admonish, guide, and counsel the members in their duties and responsibilities. They show us wherein we may correct our lives and make necessary preparation for our temporal as well as spiritual salvation.

In addition to the events of the future in the form

[17a]Doc. & Cov. 76:5-10.

of signs still to be fulfilled (Chapters Two, Three and Four), the second coming of Christ is the greatest event of which the prophets have spoken. The revelations of our dispensation have all suggested the nearness of the event. It is apparent that Jesus will make three appearances, one to his people, a second to the besieged Jews, and the last to the world in great power and glory.

The millennium as a period of promise for the honorable of the earth, including the heathen nations, has already been mentioned. The end of the world occurring at the second coming of Christ means the end of moral wickedness on the earth, but life continues on the earth. Many wonderful privileges and opportunities await the faithful mortals during this era. The gathering of His Saints will be by appointment to designated areas just before "the arm of the Lord fall(s) upon the nations."[17] All Saints should look continuously to the leadership of the Church for guidance and instruction. (Chapter Five.)

As indicated in this chapter, Satan will be loosed for a short season toward the end of the millennium, and the last great battle between the forces of good and evil will result. Satan and his followers will be cast into outer darkness to remain forever. The earth will then become celestialized as the habitat of celestial beings, while other resurrected persons will reside on some other world.

---

[17]Doc. & Cov. 45:47.

MESSAGE TWO—(B) MAN'S DESTINY

When man's body dies, his spirit enters the world of spirits to continue his education in the plan of life and salvation. There will be opportunities for further advancement on the way to perfection for those who have prepared themselves while in mortality. Happiness will be theirs in the contemplation of success thus far attained and the joy of continuing to serve in behalf of God's children in whom they were interested during mortality.

Every person will learn that what he desired while on the earth will still be his desire in the spirit world. No one's life will be changed by some magical process, but by effort of the same kind that he could have expended in mortality and won a crown of righteousness. The transition of death will not change one's character, but change we must in order to obtain the blessings of one of the kingdoms of glory as resurrected beings. This is the doctrine of "overcoming." (Chapters Seven and Ten.)

The final destiny of man following the resurrection of the body (Chapters Nine and Ten) is assignment into one of four kingdoms: Perdition (no glory) and kingdoms of glory—telestial, terrestrial, or celestial. This will be done only after an opportunity is afforded all to inherit the highest kingdom of which they are capable. The gospel of Jesus Christ saves all men who will obey, either in this life or in the future, except those (sons of perdition) who cannot repent. (Chapters Ten and Eleven.)

The faithful of God's children will have the privilege of becoming the sons of God, even gods by obedience to the higher laws and ordinances of the gospel. The powers of God are bestowed upon these only. (Chapter Eleven.)

As concerning salvation, the gospel of Jesus Christ is neither narrow nor intolerant, for all shall be saved in accordance with the laws which are lived.

Message Three—Evidences of Life Hereafter

One of the principal messages of the Church of Jesus Christ of Latter-day Saints is the fact that there is a consciousness of the spirit at death of the body, and that the resurrection of the body is an assured fact. The Doctrine and Covenants as a principal book of scripture testifies to a large part of that message.

Some of the major items of evidence, at least representative types, have been cited in this series of chapters. For purpose of convenience the chapter number and the evidence given in these chapters are shown below:

> The existence of evil spirits (Chapter Six.)
> Testimonies of ancient prophets concerning the spirit world (Chapter Six) and the resurrection (Chapter Nine.)
>
> Visitation to the spirit world by Jedediah M. Grant (Chapter Seven.)

Visit of departed dead to Parley P. Pratt while in mortality (Chapter Seven.)

Vision of the Savior's sojourn in the spirit world by Joseph F. Smith (Chapter Seven.)

Visions of the resurrection by Joseph Smith and Wilford Woodruff (Chapter Ten.)

Sight-knowledge of God and Jesus. (Chapter Eight.)

Appearances of resurrected beings. (Chapter Eight.)

Acquaintanceship with angels. (Chapter Eight.)
Book of Mormon as a witness. (Chapter Eight.)

In addition, the unreasonableness of rejecting the resurrection because the knowledge of how a resurrection occurs (when there are so many things about us which cannot be explained) is pointed out by example. (Chapter Nine.)

A TESTIMONY

Above all else, as indicated in Chapter Eight, the greatest evidence to any individual is the personal witness by the Holy Ghost. When this spirit speaks to one's soul there is no mistaking either the source of the revelation or the reality of the experience. On matters relating to the future life, every fibre of one's being is aware of its reality. Doubt and uncertainty flee and in their place are assurance and "peace in this world," with a hope of "eternal life in the world to come."[18]

---

[18]Doc. & Cov. 59:23.